For the Love of ~~Money~~ God

For the Love of ~~Money~~ *God*

A Christian's Guide to
Money, Marriage, and Miracles

Mike Richardson

Dedication

I dedicate this book to Samuel and Ruth Richardson, for whom I began this project.

God used Betty Owen and my momma, as well as Daniel Thornton and Larry Burkett, in a very special way to teach me the things I have written in these pages.

This book was born as the result of a church service at *Monte del Señor* Church, and Pastor Alex Corzo has consistently reminded me to keep writing. For that, I will be forever grateful.

It is of utmost importance that I mention my wife, Pam. She has lived these life experiences with me. She has truly made my God her God. She has willingly followed me to the ends of the earth (well, at least to the end of the paved road) in keeping her promise to go where I go.

Table of Contents

Introduction

When my son Samuel moved to Sinaloa at age twenty, there were still topics related to finances, which I desired to review with him. I began writing emails to him on a variety of topics related to finances and the family. I quickly realized that these topics would likely benefit many others—young and old alike. This book has been born out of those emails between Samuel and me.

I believe that one of the most important principles related to finances is *contentment*. I, like most people, have had many struggles in this area. For decades, my most consistent challenge has been the condition of our vehicles. We live about an hour off the paved road so our vans take a tremendous beating on the dirt roads.

This weighed heavily on my heart for many years. It was always in the forefront of my mind. God used our vans and a car wreck to teach me lessons that I really needed to learn about *contentment* and *trust*.

I would like to share with you a letter I wrote in response to a man whom I had never met; he was offering us a van.

Dear Dave:

I am sitting here trying to type my response through the tears that keep welling up in my eyes.

Over the last nine years, we have tried to depend completely on the Lord for all of our needs—both personal and ministry. I have seen God provide all the resources that we needed to work here in Mexico.

My personal income has averaged less than $10,000 per year since we have been in Mexico, yet God provided over $30,000 last year to cover the cost of my wife's illness.

When we needed to start doing our printing, He provided all the equipment. When I needed a helper, He sent Nathan here to work with me.

When Pam was expecting our fourth child, Samuel, over fourteen years after our third child, she asked if we could use disposable diapers. I told her I did not know, but that if God provided enough money to buy them, then we would use them. Well, while she was pregnant, almost everyone who gave us something for the baby gave us disposable diapers. Samuel was over one year old before we had to buy the first diaper.

My son Michael had a doctor's appointment that was going to cost 3,000 pesos (at the time the peso was 3 pesos = 1 USD); we were 317 pesos short of having enough. No one knew we were short of funds. Nevertheless, the day before his appointment, a man came up to me after church and gave me 300 pesos that another man had given him to give to me. The giver had said he wanted to help with the doctor's visit. After talking a little while, the man started to leave and then abruptly turned around. He said, "I almost forgot, his daughter wanted to help too." He handed me a plastic baggy full of change.

When I got home and counted the money, it was exactly 17 pesos!

That appointment was to treat a disease that US doctors did not know how to treat at that time. My son was in a wheel chair—now he walks!

The area that has caused me to struggle repeatedly is our vehicles. Every time our van breaks down, God has provided a way to fix it. No member of my family has ever been hurt because of a problem with our vans. Yet things have happened that have caused me great concern. A few include:

My wife, while riding with our five young children, lost the brakes while going down a steep dirt road in the mountains. About half way down, she was able to go up a narrow entrance to someone's house and coast to a stop. God protected her!

Another time, the upper A-frame cracked while I was driving, causing the right front tire to lay down flat on the road. I was driving 60 mph at the time. Despite the traffic, I was able to aim the car to the side of the road and slide to a stop without hitting anyone. God protected the 12 people in the van. No one was hurt!

Time after time, the Lord has protected us and provided mechanics in the right place at the right time. Yet, I have struggled emotionally and spiritually—sometimes thinking that the Lord has forgotten me in this area. I would cry out to God asking for something in better condition. His answer was always for me to have patience and trust that He would provide all my needs. God constantly reminded me that if I did not have something that I thought I needed, it was not His will or not His timing. Nonetheless, I struggled tremendously in the area of vehicles.

Finally, I came to an inner peace about vehicles. I realized, I mean, realized deep within my spirit that if I could trust God for medical needs, ministry needs, and even diapers, that I could trust Him for vehicles too. For the first time in years, I had peace in my heart about driving older vans.

Now, you offered me a van that is 10 years newer than what we have. Yes, we can use the van and would love to accept it!

I accept it as God's provision for my family, not as something I think that I deserve. I accept it now, realizing that God is much more concerned with the inner man—our thoughts, our attitude, and our motives—than He is with the outward appearances, like the condition of our car.

God has taught me a lot over these years with my vans—more than I could have ever learned had he provided a new van years ago when I thought that I needed it.

Thank you very much for allowing God to work through you in this way.

In Christ,
Mike

Out of Control

Returning from a nine-day trip, to Jocotitlan, a city in southern Mexico, we stopped at a friend's house to pick up our mail. I returned to the van, which was parked on the side of an access road. While looking through the mail, I heard tires squealing and looked up to see a full-size car that had lost control and hit a motorcycle rider. The car spun out of control—jumping the curve at 30 mph—heading straight for our van.

I yelled, "Hold on!" Then I braced myself for the impact. The face of the young man driving the car looked terrified as his car bore down on us. At that moment, 7:15 pm on December 23, 1995, I saw God's hand at work in our life once again.

The car stopped less than one inch from my door! Later, I realized that my finger would not even fit between his car and mine.

When preparing to leave Jocotitlan, we had prayed that God would send angels to watch over us. He truly did. That car could not have stopped in such a short distance without the hand of the living God intervening.

As I climbed out the van window, I saw the motorcyclist lying in the street. I ran to the nearest house and told them to call the police. When I returned to the motorcyclist, I was the first one to reach him.

He lay broken and twisted—almost lifeless. A doctor who was driving by stopped to help. We gently turned the motorcyclist over and dislodged his tongue from his throat. The doctor held his tongue with a comb. Kneeling beside him, I prayed as we waited for the ambulance. The doctor did an emergency tracheotomy and inserted the casing of a Bic pen to hold it open, then told me to hold it while he began to check other things.

When the medics arrived, I continued helping with the air tube they inserted. Finally, he was prepared for transporting to the hospital. We moved him to a board to protect his back, then to the gurney, and finally to the ambulance.

I went to a nearby house, washed the blood from my hands, and cried. Life is short. Sometimes shorter than we think. As this young man lay in the street with his life ebbing away, my biggest concern was not whether he would continue to live in this life or not. It was that he would regain consciousness long enough to hear the gospel before he stood before our Lord and Savior to give an account of his life.

After several days, I found out that the name of the motorcyclist was Elias Zapata. I went to the hospital to see him and his family. He was 21 and his wife, Claudia, was only 16. They had been married one month. Elias had a broken jaw and arm; both legs were crushed. When I arrived, he was still in a coma.

Over the next few weeks, many things transpired that transformed my outlook on life. I visited Elias at the hospital three times. Each time he remained comatose. One day, I received word that he had regained consciousness and was being transferred to another hospital. I decided to wait a few days so he could regain his strength, then I would go and visit him.

Several days later, I went to visit him at the new hospital. At the information desk, they said that he was no longer at their hospital. After further questioning, they told us that he had died. The chance to share the Gospel with him was gone.

César and I spent several hours looking for his house. We visited his wife, mother, and mother-in-law. We were able to share the Gospel with them. His widow, Claudia, seemed most open to the Gospel.

The timing and results of this situation have caused me to do more soul-searching than any other single event since we moved to Mexico. I believe that God is trying to teach me to know and do His will for the salvation of men.

The boy who was driving the car that hit Elias contacted me through a friend. His name is Fernando. I spent three hours sharing the Gospel with him.

I had just finished reading a book called *The Missionary Problem*, written in 1901 by a leading English minister in response to a mission conference in 1900. It was a call to prayer and personal sacrifice in order to support missions both in personal service and in giving. Its message is amazingly clear and straightforward. It is just as applicable today as it was in 1901. I have seen within myself a greater need for personal sacrifice in both my time and resources.

I was reading the account in Mark chapter ten about the one who asked Jesus what he must do to inherit eternal life. Jesus said that he should sell everything, give to the poor, and take up the cross and follow Him.

Twenty-eight years ago, I wrote in my Bible, "Do I lack this? Would I be willing to give up my home and cars to go to the mission field?" As I was reading, I thought, I guess that I do not lack it since I am on the mission field. However, I believe that the Lord is showing me that I, like most Believers, need a greater level of personal sacrifice.

Many die every day who have not heard of, nor received our Lord. We must tell the people of His love for them.

We must call all who are under our influence to a deeper service—a complete sacrifice of self and personal belongings—for the advancement of the Kingdom of God. If we do not call them to this commitment, then who will?

> For the wages of sin is death, but the gift of God is eternal life in Christ Jesus our Lord.
>
> — Romans 6:23

We have a choice to make that no one can make for us.

> That if you confess with your mouth the Lord Jesus and believe in your heart that God has raised Him from the dead, you will be saved. For with the heart one believes unto righteousness, and with the mouth confession is made unto salvation.
>
> — Romans 10:9-10

Ask yourself this question: Are there people in my life that, if they died today, could stand before God and say, "But (your name) did not tell me of Your love. How was I to know?"

The words of a song keeps ringing in my ears.

> How will they hear? How will they know?
> Who is going to tell them if we do not go?
> Living in darkness, lost and in sin
> Who is going to tell of His love for them?
> From the desert Sahara to the South China Sea
> There are millions who still have not heard
> Of the love that He has given so we could receive
> The salvation revealed in His Word.

How will your coworkers, the store clerk, or the boy next door hear if you do not tell them? We must live every day as though it were our last. This short life will soon be over, and we will be standing before our Lord. Our primary purpose is to continue the work that our Lord started—bringing souls into the Kingdom.

Mike Atkins says in his book, *Church of the Nations*, "We are called to people—wherever they physically live. We cannot measure our progress by lines on a map. We can only mark our progress one human heart at a time—as each one turns from death to life in Jesus' name."

We must learn to know and do God's will for the salvation of men.

A Knock on the Door

One day, there was a knock on the door. Pam answered to find yet another person asking for help. She told her that we did not have money to give her, but we could give her some food.

The woman then raised her fist as if to hit Pam. At that moment, just before striking Pam, she fell backwards and hit the ground. Pam ran into the house to get me.

I went out to check on her. She was lying on the ground alternating between convulsing and grabbing handfuls of grass then shoving it into her mouth. After she returned to herself, we spent time sharing the Gospel with her. When we told her the plan of salvation, she said that she had never done anything wrong in her life and did not need a redeemer!

She left our house, strolled to the next house, knocked on the door, and asked them for money.

There is spiritual warfare everywhere, for the hearts, lives, and souls of people. Our goal, our high calling, must be for the salvation of men. Progress is made one life at a time.

Contentment and *trust*—those are the keys to knowing and doing God's will. It is my hope and my prayer that God will take this book and these stories about the work that He has done in our lives and use them to bless you, encourage you, and help you grow in your relationship with Him. Let God and His Word mold your thoughts, your attitudes, and your actions into the image of Christ.

Remember that the way you handle finances is simply an outward indicator of your inward relationship with God. Get right with God, and then ask Him to help you with your finances!

Chapter 1

Prosperity or Poverty

As Believers, does God offer us prosperity and affluence, or poverty and lack?

The study of how the Bible relates to money and possessions will likely be one of the most profitable studies in the life of a Believer. Most of the time, money and our handling of money is simply an outward indicator of what is happening in our lives spiritually.

God promises that we, as Believers, can have a peace that passes all understanding. Yet too often, we do not have peace in the area of finances. The primary reason for this lack of peace is due to the lack of understanding about money and finances from a Biblical perspective, as well as the lack of training in the proper handling of the resources that God has placed in our hands.

Larry Burkett states that there are nearly 700 direct references to money in the Bible and that nearly two-thirds of all of the parables that Christ taught dealt with the use of money. Those two facts alone show us that the use, or misuse, of the resources that God has placed in our hands is very important!

In most marriages, money is the worst area of communication, but it does not have to be that way. If you filter financial decisions through the Word of God, then your finances will become an area of wonderful communication between husband and wife. However, you must understand the Biblical principles of finances for that to happen.

God Is More Concerned with Your Attitude Than With Your Bank Account!

The abundance of money or the lack of money does not affect your relationship with the Lord—only your attitude toward the resources, or lack thereof.

I believe that the key to success in our finances involves three key principles that we should all learn to live by:

1. Earn as much as you can without neglecting your other responsibilities.
2. Give generously all the time. Give sacrificially, without hesitation, when the Lord leads you to do so.
3. Save the rest. God frequently provides what we need ahead of time. Save for those unexpected circumstances that will certainly arise in your life.

While God does occasionally provide for your needs in a miraculous way, that is not the norm. God does not just miraculously give you all that you need. You must work to meet your needs and the needs of your family. Work is hard and requires effort on your part.

> In the sweat of your face you shall eat bread till
> you return to the ground, for out of it you were
> taken; for dust you are, and to dust you shall return.

—Genesis 3:19

"In the sweat of your face you shall eat bread till you return to the ground." Adam was also to tend the garden before the fall.

> Then the LORD God took the man and put him in
> the garden of Eden to tend and keep it.

—Genesis 2:15

Work is not part of the curse! Sweat may be part of the curse, but work is a blessing from the Lord. No matter how much or how little you earn, having a way to work and earn money is a blessing from the Lord.

The Bible does not ever talk about retirement (ceasing to work). There is never a time in the life of a healthy Believer that we should stop working. Your work on earth should not end until the day you die. While it is true that your work may change as you get older, your work does not stop! Retirement is not a Biblical concept.

The one exception to this principle was for the Levites who worked in the temple. At the age of fifty, they ceased doing the primary work in the temple but they continued to help the younger ones in carrying out the work.

> **And at the age of fifty years they must cease performing this work, and shall work no more.**
>
> **—Numbers 8:25**

Again, your work may change as you age, but the healthy Believer's work should not cease until the day he goes to be with the Lord.

When God discusses wealth, the topic does not only relate to money and finances, it encompasses much more.

Your most important treasures are in heaven. If what you are doing today will be of no value to God in 1000 years, then perhaps it is not of much value today. It is not what you have that is important; it is what you are doing with what you have that is important.

Material things are the result of doing our work well. Do your work well and you will be blessed with a good name. The result of having a good name will bring blessing upon the name of the God whom you serve. It may also bring about a material blessing in your life.

Wealth and Our Creative Ability Are Related

Your wealth—the resources in your hands—are actually an extension of your personality. You can use your wealth, like your personality, creatively for spreading the gospel, or you can waste it on frivolous activities. Your wealth can corrupt (i.e., paying bribes) or it can build up (bringing others to Christ).

The Blessing of the Lord Makes One Rich

A few years ago, I was looking for a truck. My mechanic in Arteaga told me about someone who had three almost new vehicles for sale. He took me to look at them. They were new and had very few miles on them. Since he was driving an older truck, I asked him why he did not drive a newer one. He told me that he was afraid someone would stop him and take it away from him on the highway.

The unsaved have fear about losing their positions but God tells the Believer that he gives His blessings to enrich our lives and that His riches do not add sorrow to our life.

> The blessing of the LORD makes one rich, and He adds no sorrow with it.
>
> —Proverbs 10:22

Everything you own will be left behind when you die. Yet so many people struggle their whole lives to accumulate possessions. Many times that struggle is to the exclusion of everything else.

Why is it that way?

Does it have to be that way?

> But the day of the Lord will come as a thief in the night, in which the heavens will pass away with a great noise, and the elements will melt with fervent heat; both the earth and the works that are in it will be burned up. Therefore, since all these things will be dissolved, what manner of persons ought you to be in holy conduct and godliness, looking for and hastening the coming of the day of God, because of which the heavens will be dissolved, being on fire, and the elements will melt with fervent heat?
>
> —2 Peter 3:10-11

The world can give you material things and you may be miserable, worried, or frustrated.

God wants to give you true riches, which do not include these sorrows.

You must be willing to turn over your finances to God—how they are being managed; how they are being multiplied; how they are being used to advance the Kingdom of God.

Learn to Trust Him with Every Aspect of Your Life

Do not focus your hopes on material things. Focus your hope on being transformed by the renewing of your mind.

> Do not lay up for yourselves treasures on earth, where moth and rust destroy and where thieves break in and steal; but lay up for yourselves treasures in heaven, where neither moth nor rust destroys and where thieves do not break in and steal. For where your treasure is, there your heart will be also.
>
> —Matthew 6:19-21

Regardless of how much money you have, you must live a different life, one that is completely dedicated to the Holy One.

You can have a peace that passes all understanding. When things go well, live in peace. When things go badly, live in peace.

Wealth is neither moral nor immoral. There is no inherent virtue in poverty. Riches do not indicate our spirituality. A lack does not make you spiritual. Abundance does not make you spiritual. We must be faithful to give glory to God in all aspects of life, including our finances.

> He who trusts in his riches will fall, but the righteous will flourish like foliage.
>
> —Proverbs 11:28

Our primary focus should never be on our finances or on how much money we are earning. We should look to God for spiritual blessings in all that we do—school, work, home, church.

> But seek first the kingdom of God and His right-
> eousness, and all these things shall be added to
> you.
>
> —Matthew 6:33

Producing wealth is implied as something positive in the life of the Believer when the Bible talks about the spiritual gift of giving. However, you must always remember that it is about your attitude toward the provision that God has entrusted to you. Do not trust in what you have; trust in Him whom you serve!

> Command those who are rich in this present age
> not to be haughty, nor to trust in uncertain riches
> but in the living God, who gives us richly all
> things to enjoy.
>
> —1 Timothy 6:17

The key to a right relationship with the Lord is integrity in handling your finances—the possessions that the Lord has placed into your hands.

> The integrity of the upright will guide them, but
> the perversity of the unfaithful will destroy them.
> Riches do not profit in the day of wrath, but right-
> eousness delivers from death.
>
> —Proverbs 11:3-4

God Does Not Condemn Wealth

God does not condemn the wealthy. God does not condemn the accumulation of possessions.

The things that you have are not important. The utility that they give you is the important factor. Too often people are hung up on material things—not God. Are not the cares of the day sufficient for themselves?

God owns it all; we are stewards. Without a doubt, one second after you die you will understand this concept. However, you need to understand it now.

You need to become a better steward of what God has entrusted to you. You must not forget the example of the unfaithful steward. Everything that he had was taken away. Ask yourself, "Am I a good of a manager of the things that God has entrusted to me?

> By humility and the fear of the LORD are riches
> and honor and life.

> —Proverbs 22:4

What Does God Expect from You?

What does God expect from you? As you acknowledge God in all of your ways, He will guide you and direct you in every aspect of your life. That includes our finances!

The world has a "financial wisdom" that is different from the wisdom that comes from above! Do not lean on what you learned from the world. Lean upon the Lord. As you acknowledge Him, He will give you the wisdom and the understanding to follow the path that He has laid down for you and your family.

> Let not mercy and truth forsake you; Bind them
> around your neck, write them on the tablet of
> your heart, and so find favor and high esteem in
> the sight of God and man. Trust in the LORD with
> all your heart, and lean not on your own under-
> standing; in all your ways acknowledge Him, and
> He shall direct your paths.

> —Proverbs 3:3-6

You Must Understand the Ways of God and Apply Them in Your Life!

As you apply God's wisdom in your life, He will pour out abundant blessings upon you and your family. Sometimes they will be financial blessings, but most of the time they will be spiritual blessings.

Earn as much as you can without neglecting your other responsibilities. Give generously all the time. Give sacrificially, without hesitation, when the Lord leads you to do so. Save the rest.

God frequently provides what you need ahead of time. Save for those unexpected circumstances that will certainly arise in your life.

Use discretion in every aspect of your life. Spend with discretion. The fact that it is on sale does not mean that it is a good buy or that it is the correct time to buy it. Steak may be on sale this week at the grocery store, but if you are living on a beans and rice kind of budget, you still cannot afford the steak. Every September, last year's model cars go on sale. But that fact does not mean you can afford to buy one, or that you should buy one.

Give with discretion and know when not to give.

- Is the need at hand one that God is calling you to meet?
- Is the need due to the person's own lack of responsibility?
- Is this a situation where God is bringing discipline into that person's life?

Understand the Situation

Understand the situation, then use wisdom and discretion in determining whether or not you are responsible to meet this need. Do not rush into making a decision too hastily. Do not wait once you understand the will of the Lord.

There was a time when my wife and I were saving to buy a newer car. We were committed to living debt free, so each month we set aside a certain amount of money to put toward the purchase of a vehicle. As we were getting close to the amount of money needed to buy a car, my excitement grew. Finally I would be able to get rid of that old clunker that I had been given!

I was working as a Chief Financial Officer at the time but I was driving a car that someone had given me under the condition that I would haul it out of his yard. A little work got it running again, but it really was an old car—about thirty years old. The seats were almost destroyed. The paint was peeling off from the sun. Nevertheless, I got it running and used it for my daily transportation.

My reserved parking space was next to the front door—right beside the reserved spot where the owner parked his new Mercedes! The men in the factory would make jokes about my car. They frequently asked things like, "Doesn't Chuck pay you enough to buy a decent car?" My answer was always the same. "My car is paid for; how about yours?"

I must admit that there were times that my pride would get to me and I was embarrassed about the car. I remember one time, when it was hot, I was coveting a coworker's car that had air conditioning. I was going to be leaving on a long trip and I dreaded driving in the heat with no air conditioning. Her car was a make and model that I really liked. I sat in the parking lot that day and longed for a car like that one.

When I returned from my trip, that coworker had purchased a new car! When she told me about it, she said, "My car is getting old and needed a lot of repairs." She went on to tell me how the radiator's hose had developed a leak, and how, one day, the fan belt broke and left her stranded, and then how the battery had died. She told me, "I just couldn't afford all the repair costs anymore."

I did not say anything. I just silently thanked the Lord that I did not have any debt and asked Him to help me not to have a coveting heart.

It was not very long after that event that I learned of a surgical need in the life of a friend. I lay in bed for several nights thinking about all the mutual friends whom I could ask to help meet that need. I finally gave $1,000 towards the need but it was not enough. They still could not have the surgery.

As the days passed, the voice of the Lord grew stronger and stronger. "Give them your car fund!" I struggled and wrestled with doing that. I had worked hard, I had given generously, I had saved the rest for a car!

Was it really God or was it just my desire to help my friend in his time of need? The inward struggle was deep but I finally agreed to do what I knew I should have done all along. Deep inside, I knew from the beginning that it was the Lord's will.

When I mentioned it to my wife, she was instantly ready to give the gift. She was excited. Once I had worked through my mental struggles, God confirmed it through my dear wife. The decision came from us as one. Larger financial decisions should be made that way. Two people working together as one. Do not try to force your opinion on your spouse. Think about it. Pray about it. Come to a mutual agreement.

As a result of that surgery, God gave that couple a precious gift — a daughter named Abigail.

Earn as much as you can without neglecting your other responsibilities. Give generously all the time. Give sacrificially, without hesitation, when the Lord leads you to do so. Save the rest. God frequently provides what you need ahead of time. Save for those unexpected circumstances that will certainly arise in your life.

> The LORD by wisdom founded the earth; by un-
> derstanding, He established the heavens; by His
> knowledge the depths were broken up, and
> clouds drop down the dew. My son, let them not
> depart from your eyes—Keep sound wisdom and
> discretion; so they will be life to your soul and
> grace to your neck.
>
> —Proverbs 3:19-22

The lack of self-control in spending is a huge problem in the lives of many Believers. You buy what you do not need and then you do not have the funds to buy what you really need! Does your money run out before the end of the month? Have you evaluated your spending in light of your needs? Learn what a need really is and then add self-control to the knowledge that you acquire.

Back in the early 1980s, I attended a financial class taught by Daniel Thornton—a man who has since become a good friend. Even though I passed the CPA exam and was a CFO, I learned most of what I know about God's perspective on finances from him—in that class and then later on at his kitchen table as we sat and talked about life's challenges.

He taught me the self-control that comes from using the "envelope system." Each payday I took my income, dividing among the envelopes for things such as electricity, insurance, food, clothing and other bills. For example, if my car insurance cost $800 a year, I would put approximately $70 a month in the envelope. Then when it came due, I would use the money in the envelope to pay the bill. By learning not to raid the envelopes for every little whim, I was really learning self-control.

> But also for this very reason, giving all diligence,
> add to your faith virtue, to virtue knowledge, to
> knowledge self-control, to self-control persever-
> ance, to perseverance godliness, to godliness
> brotherly kindness, and to brotherly kindness love.
>
> —2 Peter 1:5-7

When we seek the Lord with a whole heart, we will obtain wisdom from Him. Along with wisdom comes riches and honor. Now it is important to remind you that, while riches do include our finances, the Bible teaches us to lay up for ourselves riches in heaven. When we obtain wisdom, God will prolong our days here on this earth. In other words, if you obtain wisdom you will live longer than if you do not obtain wisdom. Get wisdom, get understanding, and God will bless you abundantly. Part of the abundant blessing that you receive from the Lord will be a better understanding of how to handle your finances.

> Riches and honor are with me, enduring riches
> and righteousness.
>
> —Proverbs 8:18

> For by me your days will be multiplied, and years
> of life will be added to you.
>
> —Proverbs 9:11

Chapter 2

Is Money a Blessing or a Curse?

It can be either one, depending on your attitude. It can be either one, depending on your response to what God gives you. First and foremost, we must learn to be content with what we have! Godliness with contentment is great spiritual gain. While that gain might include finances, the most important part of the gain will be a deeper and fuller relationship with the Lord.

Many times, we transform a financial blessing into a curse because we take our eyes off the Lord and our relationship with Him. We must learn to flee greed and ungodly gain; we must learn to be content; we must "pursue righteousness, godliness, faith, love, patience, gentleness."

Many businessmen have fallen into sin due to financial improprieties. Many politicians have gone to jail for accepting bribes or kickbacks. Many Christians, including pastors, have been disgraced and removed from leadership due to compromises with the church's finances. It never starts out big. At first it is a small amount—just enough to get by until payday. Those little compromises begin to add up and then one day, when they are caught, they say, "I do not know how it happened!"

Well, the Bible is clear: "A little leaven leavens the whole loaf." These people rarely are overtaken in one step. Little by little, they are snared in Satan's trap. Do not be one of them. "Pursue righteousness, godliness, faith, love, patience, gentleness."

It seems that the more resources that God places in our hands, the harder it becomes not to place our faith and our confidence in ourselves and our money. Yet, you must recognize that harder does not mean impossible! You must always realize that our blessings are from the Lord!

Earn as much as you can without neglecting your other responsibilities. Give generously all the time. Give sacrificially, without hesitation, when the Lord leads you to do so. Save the rest. God frequently provides what you need ahead of time. Save for those unexpected circumstances that will certainly arise in your life.

Many times God will provide a bonus or income from an unexpected source. The typical reaction is to go home to decide what to do with the extra income. Perhaps buy new living room furniture or a new TV (one of those flat ones like you always wanted), or take a vacation since it has been years since you have gone anywhere. Then a few months later, the transmission on the car goes out or the refrigerator quits working, or the washing machine breaks and you wonder why God does not provide for the need. Perhaps, just perhaps, He did; but you spent it on something that you really did not need!

When we apply these principles to our lives, they will help us to focus on God and our relationship with Him.

> And having food and clothing, with these we shall be content. But those who desire to be rich fall into temptation and a snare, and into many foolish and harmful lusts which drown men in destruction and perdition. For the love of money is a root of all kinds of evil, for which some have strayed from the faith in their greediness, and pierced themselves through with many sorrows. But you, O man of God, flee these things and pursue righteousness, godliness, faith, love, patience, gentleness.
>
> —1 Timothy 6:8-11

Beware of the love of money! It will bring great danger in your life. Drugs, kidnapping, extortion, burglary, and robbery all have their foundation in the love of money.

Money is not the problem! It is the attitude about the money that becomes the problem! It is your attitude about money and possessions that makes it the root of all kinds of evil.

> The young man said to Him, "All these things I have kept from my youth. What do I still lack?" Jesus said to him, "If you want to be perfect, go, sell what you have and give to the poor, and you will have treasure in heaven; and come, follow Me." But when the young man heard that saying, he went away sorrowful, for he had great possessions. Then Jesus said to His disciples, "Assuredly, I say to you that it is hard for a rich man to enter the kingdom of heaven."
>
> —Matthew 19:20-23

Above all else, you must realize in the inner depths of your heart that God owns it all. If you can really get a grip on that concept, then no matter what happens, you can be content in your spirit.

If you lose everything that you have, your emotions may cry, but your spirit will know and understand that it belonged to God and that it was His right to take it away. If you can really get to the point where you understand this concept and believe it with the deepest part of your being, then, and only then, will you be free to be the steward that God desires you to be. It is freeing, it is liberating, it is amazing the relief that it will bring to your life when you realize, in the inner depths of your heart, that God owns it all!

From the time that you first accept Christ as your Savior, you are in a growth process in all areas of your life. That growth includes the area of finances. As you learn to handle what you have, the Lord will likely entrust you with more.

Money, possessions—the things that you have are a tool that God uses to help you grow in your relationship with Him. When you have a need, ask God, "What do You want me to learn?" When you have abundance, ask God, "What do You want me to learn?"

God uses your material possessions to shape you and to mold you into the image and character of Christ. If you learn to be faithful in your earthly possessions, then God will entrust to you true riches—wisdom and understanding.

If you lose your job does your peace grow or do you lose that peace that passes all understanding? Ask God, the owner of it all, what happened? What are You trying to teach me? How would You like me to deal with this?

None of us would hesitate to ask the church for prayer if we were diagnosed with cancer. We might ask for prayer about a broken transmission or a refrigerator. Yet, when we have financial struggles, we do not ask for prayer.

Why?

In large part, the church has tied financial blessings to spiritual blessings. While God occasionally blesses us financially, He places Believers at all economic levels so that we can be a testimony of His grace and of His peace—a peace that passes all understanding.

If you have a real need which is not due to mismanagement, take it to the church in prayer—without embarrassment. If you have a need that is due to the mishandling of your finances, learn what God says about money and begin to apply it in your life. Be faithful and watch God bless you as you mature and follow His principles.

Prayer Changes Things

Pam's mother, Nellie, had a stroke at her home in Atlanta. She was taken by ambulance to the hospital. Pam flew up to be with her. The day Pam arrived, her mother had another stoke. She passed away that evening.

After packing, the kids and I left at 1:30 in the morning to drive to Atlanta. While Pam was in the middle of making some difficult decisions, I was getting close to Houston, Texas—the halfway point between our house and Atlanta. Suddenly the transmission in the Suburban began to slip. While it was slipping, the RPMs increased and the engine threw a rod. We coasted to the side of the highway. Not knowing anyone in Houston, we sat there and prayed. Later, I called a pastor in Atlanta. He prayed with us and the Lord began to put into place the circumstances that brought relief to the situation.

A friend in Mexico called to see how our trip was going. When I explained the situation, he said he would pray. After he hung up, he called his brother-in-law in Dallas. In turn, he called a pastor in north Houston. The pastor called his son and he came to south

Houston to pick up our trailer and us. He towed our trailer and took us to the church. The pastor fed us, gave us a place to stay, and loaned us a van to look for a new car. (The suburban was damaged beyond repair.) Later that evening Samuel said, "We spent six hours on the side of the road—one for each kid!"

Meanwhile in Atlanta, Pam and her sister, Angie, had to go ahead and make funeral arrangements. While it was very frustrating for me not to be able to be with her during this difficult time, I do understand that the Lord allowed those circumstances to happen. Pam held up very well and made many wise decisions. In addition to the funeral arrangements, Pam was able to take care of many details in the house.

I began to look for a replacement vehicle—a van or a 4x4 truck. After four days, we had not found anything. On the fifth day, I bought a truck. It was very nice, a good price, and got me out of a difficult situation.

Sometimes challenging things happen that you do not understand, but you must always remember that the Lord is in control.

> His lord said to him, "Well done, good and faithful servant; you were faithful over a few things, I will make you ruler over many things. Enter into the joy of your lord."
>
> —Matthew 25:21

Develop a Lifestyle of Praying for Your Needs

There are several methods used for deciding where to dig a well. In our area, most people use Don Inez to mark a location with his divining rods. Instead of doing that, I asked Lucio to help me pick the site. After walking the entire property, he selected the drilling site. Then the drilling equipment began to dig. At two hundred eighty feet, the well diggers took a break.

While I was gone for a few days, Inez went to my property and told everyone that there would be no water where we were digging—that all the water on my property was on the other side. He left a message for me stating that I should stop drilling and pay him one thousand pesos to tell me where the water is located. I told the person that gave me the message that I believed there was water and that I would not be moving my well, nor would I pay Inez to mark a location for me.

While we were waiting for the well diggers to return, some people began to harass Lucio. They were telling him that he was causing me to waste my money. I could see that he was more than just a little concerned. I told him not to worry about it. "It is the Lord's money, land, and well." I added that I believed the Lord would provide water but that, "We will praise Him regardless of what happens." Pam and I began praying even more earnestly for water! We were not praying just for the water. We were praying that the Lord would demonstrate power for Lucio's sake.

It took the well diggers about a week to return.

Upon arriving, the owner came to me and said that it looked like we were not going to get any water. Then he added that we should get Don Inez to pick a location for us! I told him thank you for the counsel, but that I believed we were digging in the right place. With great doubts, he continued digging. I went home to pray. That afternoon, I returned to the land to see how much he had dug. When I arrived, the workers told me that they had dug less than three feet before they hit a vein of water. We had planned to dig beyond the first water source to create a reserve to hold extra water. While digging the reserve, they hit three more water veins! The Lord not only demonstrated His power, He also encouraged Lucio and me.

Many times the Lord is waiting for us to ask Him before answering a prayer. You have not because you ask not. Never forget to take your needs to Him in prayer. Develop a lifestyle of praying for your needs with your wife and your children.

Coincidence?

Let me tell you a story that happened back in the 1990s during the time before we had internet, email, or Facebook.

A few days before Christmas, I was working at my new office trying to finish the electrical wiring for our printing presses. When I started to climb a ladder, I began to feel dizzy and hot. Not being able to continue to work, I returned home.

My temperature rose to 104.5. Over the next couple of days it would drop a little and then go right back up. I shivered uncontrollably and was unable to eat. I became delirious and incoherent. I could not even stand up. I went to the shower and sank to the floor with the cold water running over me.

During the heat of this battle, Mike Farris, a friend from Virginia, called to see how we were doing. When he found out that I was sick, he hung up and called his prayer chain. Over the next couple of hours, people were praying for me. My fever began to drop. This time it did not go back up.

Was his phone call a coincidence?

NO!

Was his phone call when I was delirious a coincidence?

NO!

Was it a coincidence that, when a group of people began praying for me, my fever went down and never came up again?

NO!

This is just another example that we serve a God who is interested in every detail of our life—a mighty and a powerful God who answers our prayers.

God Is Interested in You

God is interested in every detail of your life, including your finances.

The amount you have is not important; it is your faithfulness in using what God has placed in your possession that matters. God does not condemn wealth nor does He commend poverty. He owns it all! Whatever He entrusts to you, you must hold with an open hand—the hand of a steward. Whether God gives you prosperity or poverty, your attitude should be the same—the Lord is my Redeemer and in Him, I will put my trust!

Deep down in your spirit, you know what you should do. Your faith requires action! Too many times, you do not take action because of fear, frustration, or confusion. Living your life by your feelings instead of faith in the Word of God can be very dangerous.

Ron Blue defines stewardship as the use of God-given resources for the accomplishment of God-given goals.

Many Christians have adjusted their expectations to those around them—comparing what they have to what others have. They are not thankful for what they have; they are depressed and discouraged because of what they do not have!

The key to overcoming depression and discouragement is contentment.

> Let your conduct be without covetousness; be con-
> tent with such things as you have. For He Himself
> has said, "I will never leave you nor forsake you."

> —Hebrews 13:5

Most of our worries are based on what may happen, not on what is actually happening. God is in charge of the future, not me and not you.

James is my favorite book of the Bible. It teaches how to live one's faith in a practical and straightforward manner.

> **James, a bondservant of God and of the Lord Je-**
> **sus Christ, to the twelve tribes which are scat-**
> **tered abroad: Greetings. My brethren, count it all**
> **joy when you fall into various trials, knowing that**
> **the testing of your faith produces patience. But let**
> **patience have its perfect work, that you may be**
> **perfect and complete, lacking nothing.**

> **—James 1:1-4**

There is not just a reason for the trials in your life; there is a need for the trial! Hardships help you to see your inner self. They help you to examine your life. They help you to make the needed changes in your life.

Without a doubt, they are hard to endure, but it is the enduring that makes you what you are. It forms you. It molds you. Every trial that finds its way into your life comes with intentional purpose.

God's primary business is to help Believers to become more like Christ. It takes trials and the testing of our faith to produce mature Believers. Trials are the soil in which we grow. "My brethren, count it all joy when you fall into various trials."

James does not say if trials come, but when they come. Expect them! Do not hide your face. Just because you are a Believer, you are not exempt. The rain falls on the just and the unjust alike. Satan fights us, the world opposes us, and this makes life full of struggles!

They Find You!

You do not need to make your own trials; they find you. Never-theless, sadly, many times we bring trials upon ourselves. The way we act, the way we react, even the way we eat can bring trials and struggles in our lives. The way we talk to people, our attitudes, our work habits, our money management—all have the potential of bringing trials and struggles. "My brethren, count it all joy when you fall into various trials."

The types of trials that you will face are countless—emotional trials, mental trials, physical trials. Then there are the trials that you experience as a result of living the Christian life.

There will be trials or tests that are the result of the mountaintop experiences with God. It takes special grace for those days because you tend to grow proud of your victories. When you are strong, your heart is lifted up and you tend to have the "I can do it" attitude. Your focus must be on Jesus Christ and His work in you. You can do no good apart from the work that Christ does in and through you.

Prosperity is often thought of as a blessing, but it brings many trials with it. When a man's wealth increases, many times his faith is tested. Adversity has slain its thousands, but prosperity has slain its ten thousands.

Job experienced this time of trial. Paul was intimately acquainted with trials.

Consider your response to your trials. James says to count it joy when you face them. Peter said that you should not be surprised at the fiery trials you are going through. He added that you should not even consider it something strange. Rejoice, be very glad; those are the correct responses. They make you a partner with Christ in His suffering. Oh, but that is not what we want to do. Our inner selves want to lash out at others, but God said to count it all joy when you fall into various trials.

The trials of life are not all the same; they are like the multi-colored pieces of cloth that you use to make a beautiful quilt. God arranges and mixes them into a final product that will bring Him glory.

Trials cause you to evaluate your goals and priorities. They force you to set aside old ones and make new ones.

Live for the things that matter the most. What do you value most in this life? If you value your comfort more than character, then trials will upset you. If you value the physical and the material more than the spiritual, you will never be able to count it all joy. If you live for the present and not the future, then trials will make you bitter, not better.

Sometimes we bring trials upon ourselves because we have not listened to the still, quiet voice of the Lord when He was trying to teach us to depend upon Him. Other times trials come as they did with Job.

Regardless of the reason, our response should be the same as Job's response. "When God has finished with me, I shall shine as gold" (Job 23:10). When trials come, simply look at the trial through the eyes of faith. Your outlook, without a doubt, will determine the outcome! If you want the ending of the trial to be joyful, then begin the trial with joy. "Count it all joy!" That is the hard thing!

How is it possible to rejoice in the middle of trials? How is it possible to have joy in the middle of trials? How is it possible to have the peace that passes all understanding in the middle of trials?

Trials not only test your faith, they purify your faith. If your reaction is correct, they burn away your self-will, leaving a pure vessel that brings glory to God. If your reaction is wrong, Satan rejoices because you become useless to God and others as a result of your bitterness.

God's approval of our faith is precious, because it assures us that our faith is a genuine faith. Immature people are often impatient; they want the blessings of maturity without walking the road of growth.

God develops patience and character in your life through trials! When you go through trials, when you trust God and obey Him, the result is patience and character. You can face trials with a positive attitude because you know what trials will do in you and for you! Moreover, the result will bring glory to God.

God's goal for our life is maturity. Many Christians make the mistake of trying to shelter themselves from the trials of life and, as a result, never grow up.

How can you tell who they are? They are the ones who keep experiencing the same trial repeatedly!

It is not our material resources that are going to get us through the trials of life, but our spiritual resources.

Sometimes God uses a trial to pose the question, "Which do you love more—this or Me?"

When the Believer is focusing on his relationship with the Lord, trials produce maturity, contentment, and joy. As a result, we have that peace that passes all understanding!

People often think that riches bring contentment. That is a mistake! That is impossible! Whoever seeks joy in earthly things will not find it there. Earthly things cannot satisfy our hearts.

The Christian who walks with God and looks to Him will be content. Contentment is only found in a holy life before a loving God. The peace and security that accompanies salvation gives you an assurance that you can never find in riches.

The joy of the Lord is much better than the pleasures of the world. God promises that we as Believers can have a peace that passes all understanding in every area of our lives—including our finances.

You can easily get discouraged when trials find you, and they do find you—when you least expect them. God is working in your life, even in the midst of your struggles. If the trials and struggles of life drive you to seek a deeper walk with God, you do well.

Here are a couple of stories that clearly demonstrate that prayer does change things!

Look, Baby

When we arrived in Mexico, our youngest was nearly fourteen years old. It was not for a lack of desire that we did not have any more children, God had chosen not to bless in that way.

We thought we had it figured out—that God knew we were going to Mexico and it would be hard to be there with a bunch of little children. During the next few years, Pam gave birth to six children. When the sixth one was born, the oldest was seven. I guess we were wrong about that!

My wife got pregnant and everybody was thrilled. When someone goes fourteen and a half years without a baby, everybody is going to be excited.

A few weeks later, she began to have some miscarriage symptoms and we were not so excited anymore. We went to the doctor, who sent us to have an ultrasound. All our hopes and dreams were shattered when the doctor stated emphatically, "The baby is dead. We need to do a Dilation and Curettage (D & C)." This was a conclusion that we were unable, perhaps unwilling, to accept. Nevertheless, we still had our faith in God.

I said, "No, I don't have a peace about that." We knew if the baby was dead that there would be some natural things that would happen. If they happened, we would consider it at that time.

We went home and called the primary doctor. She, too, wanted to go ahead and do the D & C. I said, "No, we will wait two weeks and see what happens." She agreed, "Okay, we will wait two weeks and do a D & C," to which I replied, "We will wait two weeks and see what happens."

Pam went on complete bedrest and I began to fast and pray. After about a week, I felt a peace in my heart. I called the doctor and said that I wanted to do another ultrasound. She said, "Okay, we will go do another one. Then we can do the D & C." I said, "Let's just take it one step at a time."

We went to do the sonogram. The ultrasound doctor did not even want to come in the room. He sent his assistant in and she put the lubricant on Pam's belly. When she put the wand on Pam's stomach, she put it down very quickly and ran out of the room.

The doctor came in and started all over again. He spoke very broken English and we spoke very broken Spanish at that time. He put the wand on her belly and then he looked up at the screen. He began to point at the screen and say in English, "Look … baby. Look … baby."

Samuel was born alive. For those of you who speak Spanish, he was born alive and is muy vivo. (He is indeed very lively and energetic.)

I am not saying that God raised him from the dead. He could have. God has the power to do that. However, he could have been a very little baby and his heartbeat was not detected by the first ultrasound. I do not know which the case is, but I do know that God saved the life of my baby!

God cares for life and death issues and so should we!

God Likes to Throw Those Things Away

God has been faithfully providing for the needs of His people since the beginning of time. Among Believers, Philippians 4:19 ("But my God shall supply all your need according to His riches in glory by Christ Jesus") is one of the most quoted verses. Yet few completely understand the fullness of this verse; many fail to see that God is actively working in their daily lives.

In the baby department at Wal-Mart, when Pam picked up each of the baby items, she began to think about the baby growing in her womb. After so many years, she longed to hold a baby—her baby— in her arms. When she was looking at the new blankets, she noticed how soft the material seemed to feel between her fingers. Rubbing them gently against her face, she continued thinking of the coming blessing—her baby. Moving along she noticed the diaper bags. There were blue ones, green ones, and pink ones. Some were solid;

others were plaid. Some had pictures of Winnie the Pooh; others had cute brown and black teddy bears.

Continuing to walk down the aisle, she noticed the diapers—disposable diapers. Picking up a pack of newborn diapers, she noticed that they were different from the kind that she had seen years before when our other children were young. There were different styles and colors for boys and girls. They had Velcro tabs so that you could open to check the contents and then re-close them. They also had cute little pictures on them. Some had ducks; others had teddy bears. The front of the diapers had a front view of the ducks and teddy bears. The back of the diapers had a cute view of the backside of the ducks and teddy bears. After carefully selecting three packs and placing them in her cart, Pam continued moving down the aisle.

Picking up a container of baby powder, she slowly lifted the white bottle with blue letters to her nose and took a deep breath. The sweet smell of cornstarch brought back so many memories of years gone by. She quickly picked up three of them and set them gently in her buggy. Noticing the pink bottles of baby lotion and the clear bottles of baby oil, she repeated the same process. After lifting them to her nose and savoring the aroma, she placed three of each in her cart.

Picking up a tube of Desitin, she once again lifted it to her nose. The sweet, unusual scent brought back more memories. Not just giggles and coos, but the cries and screams that accompanied diaper rashes. Once again, she put three of them in her cart.

Walking a little further down the aisle, her thoughts turned from her own baby to the task at hand. She had been invited to a baby shower for three women at her new church. Since she was also expecting a baby, she was especially excited to be attending a baby shower—her first in Mexico.

Later, as she arrived at the shower, a lady came up and took the three large gift bags from her hand. Looking at the things that Pam had, she said, "These things are very nice." Then she added, "But you didn't need to buy all this." Heading off to another room with the gifts, she told Pam to have a seat.

Pam sat and listened for three hours while three ladies shared three different Bible studies on the family, children and the responsibilities of women. Throughout the studies, she squirmed—trying to find a position that was comfortable for her growing belly. She continued to sip the Sprite that I had bought her earlier when she had mentioned that her stomach was upset with morning sickness. When the studies concluded, the ladies brought out the food. The drinks and desserts had become familiar. So had the tamales. The cornhusks that covered the batter made from corn flour were tinged black from reheating them on a grill. Some were filled with chicken, others had beef and pork, and a few had refried beans. The greasy fillings and the hot salsa did not sit well with Pam's upset stomach as she sat there and tried to politely eat what she had been served.

Following the shower, she was curious why she had not seen even one present being opened. Approaching a friend she inquisitively asked, "What kinds of presents did the ladies get? Why did they not open them?" Her friend went on to explain that the ladies would open them later—at home. Then she added that the people at the church had gone in together to buy each lady a single gift. At home, Pam explained to me how embarrassed she was when she found out about the gifts. She had assumed that baby showers would be the same as they were in Georgia, that everyone would bring gifts and then look on as they were opened.

A few weeks later, she was told that the ladies were planning a shower for her.

Arriving at the church, she was surprised at the number of ladies attending her shower. Her surprise would not, however, end with that. Like the previous shower she had attended, there was a Bible study given on the family. This time, much to Pam's relief, it lasted less than an hour. As the ladies were preparing to serve the food, another table was being filled with gifts the people had brought for Pam and the new baby. After everyone was served, Pam was surprised when, unlike the previous shower, she was told that it was time to open the presents. Before she even began tearing off the cute wrapping paper covered with little baby rattles from the first gift, she could tell that it was diapers—disposable diapers. When she opened them, she realized that they were very similar to the ones that she had purchased for the previous shower.

As she was being handed another gift, her mind began to drift back to a conversation with me that had taken place a few days before. She had approached me and asked, "Can we use disposable diapers when the baby is born?" After thinking for a moment about how much our income had been reduced since coming to Mexico and how much of our savings had been used to pay for ministry-related expenses, I slowly and thoughtfully responded, "I don't know if we will have enough money to buy them, but if God provides the money we can use them." Then I added, "I think that it would be good to throw those things away."

As she opened the next present, it too was a pack of newborn diapers—disposable diapers. Unlike the previous shower, it seemed like every one of the ladies had brought a present. Most of them had selected diapers—disposable diapers—to bring! They did not all bring newborn diapers though; they brought diapers—disposable diapers—of all sizes. Some had plain fronts. Others had little animals. Some had tape seals. Others had Velcro tabs.

When she arrived home with all the presents, I said, "I thought you said that they only give one gift at baby showers here."

Once all the gifts were in the house, we realized that we did not have a closet that would hold all of the diapers. (Most houses in Mexico do not have the abundance of closet space that one would find in the average house in the United States.) We decided to simply stack them up in one corner of the living room.

It was not long before Maria Elena, one of Pam's new friends, came to her and said that another group of ladies was planning a shower for her.

After arriving at Maria Elena's house, she was again surprised by the number of ladies who were present. This time, after a short Bible study, the ladies had Enchiladas Potosinas, a traditional food from the state of San Luis Potosi, which is located near the eastern cost of Mexico. Since Pam was now a little further along in the pregnancy, her stomach was feeling better. Picking up one of the bright orange, half-moon shaped enchiladas, she noticed that it had been fried and was crunchy. As she bit into it, she could tell that a lot of jalapeño peppers had been mixed with the hot melted cheese that filled the middle. Since she loved being able to once again eat the spicy food that is so typical in Mexico, she asked for the recipe. They have become one of our family's favorite foods to share with special guests. Pam not only appreciated Maria Elena's hospitality, she learned from it. We frequently make Enchiladas Potosinas when special guests are coming to visit.

As a side note, hospitality is very important in the life of a Believer. Being willing to share and sacrifice for others by being hospitable relates to finances too. It is something that we must not only practice, but that we must also teach to our children. First Peter 4:9 tells us to show hospitality one to another without grudging. When guests are going to be coming into the home, it becomes a family affair. Some cook, some clean, and others may make sacrifices like giving up their beds for a night or two.

Once, a friend, who was an elder at the church, told me, "I cannot have people over to my house as the other elders do because my house is under construction and I still have a lot of work to finish." He went on to say, "They all have big, nice houses and mine is so small." This attitude is in stark contrast to the attitude of Maria Elena or Don Poncho and Doña Amelia.

Our family went with Jose to visit his family up in the mountains. His parents lived in a small two-room wood and adobe home. They had no running water, no electricity, and no heat other than the cook fire. They have lived in this same house for over forty years.

When we arrived, a baby goat was running around the front yard. Samuel (4) and Isaac (3) fell in love with it. They were walking it, riding it, and just having a good ol' time.

Later that afternoon, I took Samuel, Isaac, and Anna on a walk through the woods. When we returned, the goat was nowhere to be found. Samuel ran around the back of the house to look for it. There he was—hanging up beside the barn! He was being skinned for lunch. The boys handled the situation very well.

Later that day as we were getting ready to leave, Doña Amelia came to us and said, "We really enjoyed your visit and would love to have you come back again. You can come for the day or you can come and spend several days with us."

She had spent most of her day cooking over an open fire and cleaning up after a bunch of people, yet at the end of the day she came to us with an open heart and a smile on her face and genuinely wanted us to return. That's hospitality!

This couple became Christians; in fact, they were two of the founding members of *La Iglesia de Baratillo*. Doña Amelia and Don Poncho, who is now in his nineties, are still as hospitable today as they were the day I met them.

Meanwhile, back to the baby shower.

After mingling and talking for a while, Maria Elena told Pam it was time to open the gifts. One by one she was handed the presents. Even though some were wrapped pretty in "baby" paper, while others were in gift bags, and still others were unwrapped; almost all of them had one thing in common—they were diapers— disposable diapers. Like the previous shower, the diapers were all different sizes and shapes. Some had plain fronts. Others had little animals. Some had tape seals. Others had Velcro tabs.

After Pam arrived home from the shower, I looked on with amazement at all the diapers—disposable diapers—that filled the car. We once again stacked them in the living room.

A few months later, while we were traveling to the eastern United States to visit family and friends, many wanted to bless us with a baby shower.

The first one was planned by Pam's family in Virginia. Much to our amazement, almost everyone brought diapers—disposable diapers. A few days later, as Pam walked into our home church for another baby shower, she was not as surprised by the quantity of disposable diapers that she received. Later, when my family had yet another shower, Pam again received many bags of diapers— disposable diapers. They were all different sizes and shapes.

Arriving home in Mexico, we once again stacked the disposable diapers in the corner of the living room. When the first stack reached the ceiling, we began a second one next to it.

A few days later, there was a knock on the door. When we opened it, Chuy Mejia was standing there with his arms full of diapers—disposable diapers. He said that he had come by to welcome us home from our trip and to bring a gift for the new baby! After stacking the diapers in the living room, he returned to his car for the rest of the diapers that he had brought. Once again, we needed to start another stack!

As the weeks passed, more friends came by and brought gifts for the baby—disposable diapers. They were all different sizes and shapes.

After Samuel was born, I told Pam, "I think that God has said that it would be okay for you to use disposable diapers." As the months passed, the stacks of diapers began to grow smaller. It was not until Samuel turned fourteen months old that Pam came to me and for the very first time said, "Mike, we are almost out of diapers. Can we buy some more?"

Now when I retell this story, I explain, "God is interested in our lives. He will provide for us—down to the smallest of details." I close by saying, "I think God has demonstrated that He, too, likes to throw those things away!"

Trials Find You!

Trials do find you when you least expect them. You need to prepare financially for those unexpected issues. That is why it will be important to include an emergency fund in your budget. The best way to do this is to "expect the unexpected." If you do that, you will find yourself prepared to handle most issues that arise. Therefore, part of your preparation for trials is in the area of finances—creating a fund from which you can draw when needed. However, the most important part is spiritual preparation. Develop your relationship with the Lord through reading the Word and praying. That will give you the inner peace that passes all understanding in the midst of your trials.

Our lives must be different. We must not walk the path that the rest of the world walks. We must get out there and mark the trails for others to follow. I propose that there is only one way to do that—knowing God in a deep intimate way. The only way to really know God, the only way to really mark the paths for others, the only way to really make an impact on the lives of those around us, is to get on our knees. Remember that our prayers are our way of talking to God and that He talks to us through His Word. Converse with God every day of your life.

Prayer does change things!

Chapter 3

God's Plan for a Family

What is God's financial plan for a family? Spend less than you earn and do it for a long time. Then you will be financially stable and able to give generously.

Typically, money is either the best or the worst area of communication in a marriage. Sadly, for most couples, it is the worst area of communication. Make the decision, from the very beginning, to make it your best area of communication.

The Role of the Wife

Proverbs 31 describes the excellent wife—the helpmeet that all men need. Once a couple has children, the wife's primary responsibility is most likely in the home. It is for that reason that you must learn to live on one salary. One way, perhaps the best way, to prepare for the blessing of children, and for a lifestyle that allows the mother to focus on the primary responsibility of her home, is that if both husband and wife work prior to having children, then all of the wife's income should be saved, used toward one-time purchases, or given generously. If you develop a spending plan that includes two incomes, then when the first baby comes along, financial pressures will be great with the loss of her income.

There is no specific Biblical principle that prohibits women from working or from earning money. It is important to note that Proverbs 31 verses 16 and 24 describes the excellent wife's business ventures that she did along with her household duties. However, since children require parenting, and households require management, it seems easier and more practical to manage that huge task if a wife and mother is not working full-time outside the home.

Since Titus 2:5 tells us that women should be workers at home, I believe that the fountain of any income produced by the wife should flow forth from her work in the home. Yes, I know that many will disagree with me on this point. However, God's Word does tell us that the making of a home is a task delegated to wives, so a wise woman will make this job her primary focus.

> **To be discreet, chaste, homemakers, good, obedient to their own husbands, that the word of God may not be blasphemed.**
>
> **—Titus 2:5**

While this verse does not state that women must be only homemakers, great homemaking is a full-time job in itself, and women who do not allocate enough time to it will face a significant challenge in fulfilling this responsibility well.

Titus 2:4 speaks of husband and children: "That they may teach the young women to be sober, to love their husbands, to love their children." It appears that women who do not have husbands and children will have more time available to work outside the home since the homemaking tasks will not require as much time when there is no husband or children.

I firmly believe that most wives should begin their married life as homemakers and as a helpmeet to their husbands. When Mom is home, she can devote her energy to the home, blessing the family in ways that we cannot fathom. It is not just a single blessing; it is exponential.

Stewardship

The key to understanding God's will in finances is the proper understanding of stewardship. The dictionary defines a steward as one who manages another's property. As I mentioned before, Ron Blue defines stewardship as the use of God-given resources for the accomplishment of God-given goals.

An example of a steward is a banker. He does not own your money. He cannot void a check you wrote. He cannot buy a house with your money. He does have some rights though; he can invest your money reasonably. Nevertheless, he must be willing and able to give it back when you require it of him.

Just like the banker, you are simply a steward of God's property while you are living here on the earth. God can choose to entrust you with a lot or with a little. The resources belong to Him. He can do what He desires with His resources. It is imperative you understand that you never take ownership of the things that God has entrusted to you. You are a steward. You are simply managing God's property for Him. As a steward, you must not only understand the will of God, you must also do it. A tremendous freedom comes from knowing, understanding, and believing that God owns it all. If you accept the role of a faithful steward, then God will entrust to you even more.

Tithing is an important principle. It not only shows you that you are faithful in a very small thing that God has asked you to do, but it also lays the foundation for a lifetime of blessings.

The concept of tithing is so important that I will cover it by itself in a later chapter. For now, let it suffice for me to say, why would God entrust more to an unfaithful steward?

Until a Christian recognizes God's ownership, he will not be able to experience God's direction fully in financial matters.

Worry, frustration, anger, and fear frequently come when there seems to be a lack of income—when the paycheck ends before the month ends. This is when a husband and wife will frequently begin to fuss, fight, and argue. You must come to understand that worry, frustration, anger, and fear do not come from financial problems; they are spiritual problems. Get right with God and put things back into the perspective of eternity.

Money is the outside visible indicator of what is going on inside spiritually. When the urgent things overwhelm the important things in your life, something is wrong with your life. Seek God with your whole heart every day of your life.

No Believer would say, "I don't trust God." Nevertheless, if you cannot trust Him in the little things, like money, you cannot trust Him.

You must realize that the prerequisite of peace is trust. "Trust in the Lord with all your heart. Lean not on your own understanding. In all your ways, acknowledge Him." If you trust in your job, it can let you down. If you trust in your savings and your possessions, they can let you down. Do you trust God, or do you just say that you trust God? There is a big difference!

"God, I really want to serve you, but _____" (fill in the blank). Is there any area of your life that you are holding back? God does not ask you to do unreasonable things. Give your all to Him and He will give you life more abundantly. If you want the peace that passes all understanding, learn to trust God.

Money in Marriage

God uses money in a Christian marriage to show you your strengths and your weaknesses and to teach you how to depend fully upon Him. He also uses money as a communication tool. He wants every husband to talk openly and honestly with his wife about finances. You must keep in mind that Satan wants to drive a wedge between husband and wife. He desires to break down your communication. His most common tool is money and spending. Do not ever allow frustration and fighting to arise in your marriage. Recognize it for what it is: Satan trying to attack the foundation of our society—the union of one man and one woman for life. If contentions arise in your marriage, choose to stop them. Develop a deep, loving communication with your wife.

In a practical sense, that means that you must decide what kind of house you can afford, what kind of car you can drive, how much you can spend on food, how much you can spend on clothes, how much you can spend on entertainment, telephone, internet, kitchen appliances, and everything else. However, the key is that you do it together!

As you begin to talk about the day-to-day things, you will learn a lot from each other.

It is a common misconception that it is normally the wife that "blows the budget." Most of the time, this is simply not true. The wife may buy a dress or some steaks that stretch the budget, but it is the husband who generally "blows the budget" when he goes out on a whim and buys a car, or a TV, or that new phone that he just had to have. Give grace to your wife and hold yourself to a higher accountability.

Criticizing and complaining can undermine the trust that your spouse has in you. It will cause them to see you as negative and disloyal—perhaps worse.

You may think, "I was only offering constructive criticism." That is like saying that your wife is pleasantly plump! Both are a play on words. Neither is helpful. There is no such thing as constructive criticism.

There is absolutely no place in your marriage for what some people call constructive criticism. Constructive means to build up. Criticism is to tear down. Those two words do not go together.

Think before you speak. Be kind. Build up your spouse. Be tenderhearted.

In Chapter 9, I will talk about other areas related to a family financial plan (budget).

Being Faithful

For the kingdom of heaven is like a man traveling to a far country, who called his own servants and delivered his goods to them. And to one he gave five talents, to another two, and to another one, to each according to his own ability; and immediately he went on a journey.

Then he who had received the five talents went and traded with them, and made another five talents. And likewise he who had received two gained two more also. But he who had received one went and dug in the ground, and hid his lord's money.

After a long time the lord of those servants came and settled accounts with them.

So he who had received five talents came and brought five other talents, saying, "Lord, you delivered to me five talents; look, I have gained five more talents besides them." His lord said to him, "Well done, good and faithful servant; you were faithful over a few things, I will make you ruler over many things. Enter into the joy of your lord."

He also who had received two talents came and said, "Lord, you delivered to me two talents; look, I have gained two more talents besides them." His lord said to him, "Well done, good and faithful servant; you have been faithful over a few things, I will make you ruler over many things. Enter into the joy of your lord."

Then he who had received the one talent came and said, "Lord, I knew you to be a hard man, reaping where you have not sown, and gathering where you have not scattered seed. And I was afraid, and went and hid your talent in the ground. Look, there you have what is yours."

But his lord answered and said to him, "You wicked and lazy servant, you knew that I reap where I have not sown, and gather where I have not scattered seed. So you ought to have deposited my money with the bankers, and at my coming I would have received back my own with interest. So take the talent from him, and give it to him who has ten talents. For to everyone who has, more will be given, and he will have abundance; but from him who does not have, even what he has will be taken away. And cast the unprofitable servant into the outer darkness. There will be weeping and gnashing of teeth."

—Matthew 25:14-30

In this parable, Christ compared the Kingdom of heaven to "a man traveling to a far country, who called his own servants and delivered his goods to them." Just like the heroes of faith listed in the book of Hebrews, you too are strangers and pilgrims on the earth. The earth is not your home. You are just passing through. While you are here, you are to do the will of the Father.

His will is very clear in two areas that relate to the life of every Believer. First, you are to make disciples. This means you are to be faithful witnesses to those around you. You are to go where the Lord leads you.

My son Samuel moved to Sinaloa, Mexico to work and study. That meant he must be a faithful witness in Los Mochis, Sinaloa. His friend, Ruth, lived in Monterrey. That meant she needed be a faithful witness in Monterrey. For both of them, that meant being content to be single. That meant serving God with their whole hearts as two single people.

One day, they were prepared to marry. With the blessing of both sets of parents, they did. That meant serving God together — wherever He might lead them. Samuel and Ruth married and are developing their financial plans together — as a family. Every single person must remember that the primary reason to marry is to be more effective for the Lord together than single.

The Bible is clear on what the Lord has called all of us to do.

> **Go therefore and make disciples of all the nations, baptizing them in the name of the Father and of the Son and of the Holy Spirit.**
>
> **—Matthew 28:19**

Too often, we know what the Lord's will is for our lives but instead of doing it we make excuses. While that certainly relates to the handling of our finances, it also relates to evangelism, our Christian walk, and much more.

No One Is Guaranteed a Tomorrow

Ligio and his wife Manuela had a house near the top of the mountain. He worked for the owner of the property in front of the church. They also had a cabin there. While Manuela had always spent most of her time up in the mountain, a few weeks before she died she came down and moved into their cabin in front of the church.

The ladies began to encourage her to come to church. She started attending. At eighty-two, she was almost blind, yet she would sit on the bench and listen attentively to everything that was said. One Sunday after church, she stood on the front porch with the other women and discussed what happens after this life. Nearing the end of the conversation, Pam told her, "No one is guaranteed a tomorrow. We must make a decision for Christ now, in this life."

That afternoon, Manuela was tired and slept much of the afternoon. Later that evening, she woke up feeling better and fixed dinner. That night she and her husband went to bed. About one in the morning, Ligio woke up. When he spoke to Manuela, he realized that something was wrong — she had died in her sleep.

I wish I could tell you that she had become a Christian, but I cannot. I just do not know. She knew that salvation comes only through faith in Christ. The Holy Spirit was drawing her. I pray she yielded her will to Christ.

I Am Sorry

I did not know Lucio before he became a Christian. Nevertheless, from the stories that I have heard, he was not a very nice man. He drank a lot and did many things to his family that men who drink do. He created a very unhappy and unsafe family environment.

The day that I baptized Lucio, he stood on the side of the water-holding tank, looking at his family members and said, "I am sorry for the way that I treated you. I am sorry for what I did earlier in our marriage. I am sorry for what I did when you were a child. I was wrong. Will you forgive me?"

So many times, we as Christians recognize our sin. We know in our hearts that we have sinned. We go to God and say, "I have sinned." What does He do? He is faithful and just to forgive us of our sins. Nevertheless, someone who is offended is still out there or someone to whom we need to make restitution is still out there. That is what Lucio did when he was standing on the side of that water-holding tank.

Do What My Word Says

Lucio was the sixth Believer in our church. Herminia was one of the first. She was in her mid to late seventies when she accepted Christ. She was one of the ones who wanted to be baptized at the first baptismal service. They all did.

Just a few weeks before the baptism, someone told us about a problem that Herminia had in her life. She had not spoken with her daughter, who lived next door, for five years!

Pam and I went and talked to Herminia, separately and together, trying to get her to restore that relationship. She did not want to restore that relationship. She was offended. She had bitterness in her heart. Yet, I knew that she was going to stand up and give a public testimony of her relationship with Christ and she needed to restore her relationship with her daughter.

As I was praying, asking the Lord what to do, He said, "Do what My Word says. Take somebody with you." I responded, "Lord, I only have six Believers and they are all new Christians. Whom should I take?"

He said, "Take Lucio."

Lucio was a brand new Believer and Herminia's younger brother!

I decided to go see Lucio. I went to his house and sat down at his table. Anytime you go to someone's house, they always feed you. His wife was not there, so Lucio got up and began to fix eggs over the fire in his chimney. He served and we began to eat. I was sitting there eating slowly. I do not usually eat slowly, but I was taking my time, trying to figure out what to say.

I was sitting there thinking, "How am I going to talk to this man about going with me to talk to his sister about this problem?" Before I could say anything, Lucio looked at me and said, "The baptism is next week. What are we going to do about Herminia?"

I said, "I am glad you brought that up! That is what I came here to talk to you about today. I want you to go with me to talk to her."

He said, "Okay." We set the day and time to go.

When we arrived, the same brick wall of resistance met us. When that began to happen, Lucio walked out. I was sitting there thinking, "Thanks a lot, Lucio!"

I continued to talk to Herminia and tried to convince her from Scripture that she, as the mother and as the Christian, had the responsibility to restore the relationship and overcome the bitterness in her heart. She did not want to hear it. She said that she was the one that was hurt and she was the one who was offended.

A few minutes later, Lucio came back into the house. He brought Herminia's daughter with him! I was not upset with him after that.

As soon as she walked in, they began to hug and cry. Both of them began to say, "I am so sorry. Will you forgive me?"

Lucio, being the kind of man that he was, walked out and left them in privacy. I, being the kind of man that I am, stood there and watched for a while, but then I too walked out.

Herminia's husband, Don Santos, was 83 years old at the time. He was standing in the orchard talking with Lucio.

I walked over and said, "Santos, what do you think about this?" He got this big grin on his face. That grin told it all. He was excited. Then I looked at him and said, "There is only one thing lacking!" He looked at me as if to say, "What you are talking about? They have taken care of everything."

Santos had been coming to church and he had heard the plan of salvation a lot from me. I knew that he knew the plan of salvation, but he had never expressed any true interest in the Gospel. I said,

"There is one thing lacking. Your salvation! Are you now ready to accept Jesus as your Savior?"

He looked at me and said, "Yes, I am!"

Even though I knew that he understood the plan of salvation, I wanted to confirm it. I looked over at Lucio and said, "Lucio, explain the plan of salvation to him."

Lucio said, "I can't do that!"

I replied, "Yes, you can," and moved back a step.

Lucio began effectively explaining the plan of salvation to Don Santos.

Then I stepped back up and asked, "Don Santos, are you really, truly, ready to receive Jesus?"

He said, "Yes, I am."

I asked, "Do you want to pray in your own words or do you want someone to help you pray?"

He responded, "I would like someone to help me pray."

I looked over at Lucio and said, "Lucio, help him pray."

Lucio said, "I can't do that! I can't do that!"

As I was stepping back, I said, "Yes, you can."

Lucio stepped up and they prayed a very sincere and simple prayer. Santos was saved! Then he asked, "Can I be baptized with the rest of the Christians next week?"

I responded, "Yes, you can! You can publicly testify that the Lord has changed you!"

Do you see what happened? When Herminia was guarding bitterness in her heart, she testified that the Lord had changed her life. Her husband was hearing her words, but he was also seeing her actions. However, the very day that she got right with the Lord and her daughter, he received Christ.

Would that have happened if she had not done that? We do not know, but you and I know that receiving Christ became much easier when that Christian was right with the Lord and her daughter!

Years later, one of Herminia's daughters received Christ. Later, when she reflected back to the day that she accepted the Lord, she told Pam, "I felt like I was in a deep pit where it was very dark." Then she added, "What Mike told me lifted me out of that pit and set me in the light." As she continued talking, she said, "Instead of all the fighting that was in my family, there is now harmony."

Later Herminia's grandson and his wife received Christ. They said, "We don't want to keep living like this!"

Do you see what happened? When Lucio stepped out of his comfort zone, Herminia got right with the Lord. Then, as a result, so did her husband, her daughter, her grandson, and his wife. When you get right with God, He opens doors and begins to use you in greater ways. When you are in a right relationship with God spiritually, He uses you to win souls. The Bible tells us that he who wins souls is wise. That wisdom will overflow in every area of your life, including finances.

The first time I rode to the house of Lucio's brother, Ramón, he stood at the doorway waving enthusiastically as I drove down his driveway. He was seventy-four years old and had lived alone for more than twenty years. He became a Believer. He was very grateful to be able to join our church and worship the Lord with Lucio and Santos. Ramón shuffled when he walked and had slurred speech, yet he was always ready to come to church and sing to the Lord. For those who have seen the movie, A Man Called Norman, Ramón reminds me of Norman.

When you get in a right position financially, you are in a better position for God to use you to meet the needs of your family, the church and the saints. It is, however, important to remember that we must also be willing to give of our time in order to win others for Christ.

Sweep the Floors

The second area is just as clear as the first, when you look at the preponderance of Scripture. You are to be faithful stewards of what God has placed into your hands. That means that you recognize He owns it all and that you must hold it with open hands.

It is interesting to note that He gave to each according to his own ability. He gave one, five talents; to another, two talents; and to another, one talent. He gave to each of them according to their aptitude and their capability. I am convinced that God has entrusted many in the church with an aptitude and capability far beyond the norm in today's society. Use your God-given abilities well and He will bless you abundantly. Be slothful and lazy and you will lose what you have. Squander your abilities on fruitless living and you will find yourself living like the prodigal son. However, if you stand firm in your faith and produce consistent, sustained performance in all that God brings before you, He will bless you in ways that you cannot even imagine.

Do not be afraid to sweep the floors—even if you must put in extra hours to do so. Just as Joseph was blessed for being a faithful servant when he was sold into slavery, God will bless you when you truly learn to serve. Serve with a glad heart and God will give you a peace that passes all understanding. Use your God-given abilities to serve God and others.

You produce wealth slowly, over time. Any opportunities that come your way to "get rich quickly" are temptations from Satan. He is trying to lead you astray. Consistent, sustained performance in all that you do is what God wants from you. Your employer wants the same thing—consistent, sustained performance.

God does not ask the same of each Believer. He treats us as individuals. God has, or will, equip you for what He is calling you to do. You may feel weak and unable to carry out the calling that God has given you. That, in effect, is good. When you are weak, then He is strong. When you cannot, God can!

In 2011, I had so much pain in my body that I could not walk. My son, Samuel, carried me up the stairs as if I was his little boy instead of his father. During that time, I preached a sermon titled, "You raise me up!" In that sermon, from a wheelchair, I said, "He will lift me up to the top of the mountains in Arteaga." I knew what God had called me to do. Even when I was in that wheelchair, I knew!

Within three years of preaching that sermon, I climbed that mountain and stood on the very spot where, I believe, God will allow me to install a radio station one day.

God tells us in Romans 11:29, "For the gifts and the calling of God are irrevocable." Know your calling. Make it sure. Then move forward with everything that is within you. No regrets, no reserves. Give Him your all and He will give you life more abundantly.

God will prepare you to do what He has called you to do. When we first came to Mexico, I was still very shy. I could not speak in front of a group. When someone would ask me to speak, I was so afraid to be in the front alone that I would ask my wife, Pam, to come to the front with me. I would give her passages to read and stories to tell so that when I could not think of the next thing to say, she would fill in the gap. We did that until after Anna was born. Nevertheless, God in His wisdom and foreknowledge knew that He was calling me to pastor a church and to speak at conferences. Little by little, He began to prepare me. Then in 2011, I preached a sermon at church based on Exodus 4:12. "Now therefore, go, and I will be with your mouth and teach you what you shall say."

It was after I preached that sermon that I finally realized that God had prepared me and had placed in my hands what I needed to effectively share the Word. I no longer feel like that shy little boy when I stand in the pulpit. I now feel like the man whom Jesus called and prepared.

Be faithful and serve. One day you will realize that God has prepared you in a unique and special way to do His will. As God blesses you financially, hold your possessions with an open hand. They belong to God. You are only His steward—His manager.

Earn as much as you can without neglecting your other responsibilities.

Give generously all the time. Give sacrificially, without hesitation, when the Lord leads you to do so.

Save the rest. God frequently provides what we need ahead of time. Save for those unexpected circumstances that will certainly arise in your life.

Learn these principles. Live by these concepts.

In the parable of the talents, the master did not expect the same results from everyone. To everyone to whom much is given, from him much will be required; and to whom much has been committed, of him the master will ask the more. God has given you much—beginning with your salvation. Be a faithful servant. No matter what the cost—be a faithful servant.

While the master blessed the first and second servants, it is important to note that the third lost all that he had. He did not use it, so he lost it. You have unique aptitudes, abilities, and capability. Use them for the glory of God!

Sadly, the truth is that the servant with one talent was better than many Christians today. Many among us will take the Lord's money and put it in a retirement account or spend it and then never want to give it back! Do not let your mind go down that path. It is a path to pain and problems. Trust in the Lord with everything within you. When life is hard, you must lean heavily upon your relationship with Jesus.

The key to this parable is stewardship. The faithful servant was using his ability, managing his resources well, and then returning them to the master when asked. Now let us compare this parable to the one found in Luke.

> Then He spoke a parable to them, saying: "The
> ground of a certain rich man yielded plentifully.

> And he thought within himself, saying, 'What
> shall I do, since I have no room to store my
> crops?' So he said, 'I will do this: I will pull down
> my barns and build greater, and there I will store
> all my crops and my goods. And I will say to my
> soul, "Soul, you have many goods laid up for
> many years; take your ease; eat, drink, and be
> merry."' But God said to him, 'Fool! This night
> your soul will be required of you; then whose will
> those things be which you have provided?'"

—Luke 12:16-20

This farmer had great wealth. God does not object to someone having wealth. He tells us to store up in the good times so that we will have sufficient in the lean times.

Before coming to Mexico, after paying off all debt, we began to save the rest. We came to Mexico fifteen days after accepting the invitation. We did not raise money ahead of time. We did not ask anyone for support. How were we able to do that? We had saved in the good times in order to have sufficient in the lean times. God does not object to a savings account. His wisdom helps us to save.

So what is the difference between this parable and our saving ahead of time? Attitude! It is all about attitude. In the parable, the farmer was laying up for himself treasures on earth so that he could retire and live the "good life." Retirement is not a Biblical concept. We are not here to live a life of ease. We are here to fight a spiritual battle for the hearts, lives, and souls of men. Do not be found wanting in this area. Fight the good fight. Be counted faithful until the end.

Many are doing the same thing in Christianity as this farmer was doing. God rebuked the farmer and required his life that very night.

I do not believe that the farmer took one big step into that sin. I believe that throughout the years, he likely allowed himself to make little compromises that, when combined, allowed him to take that last step toward destruction. Be careful of the little compromises. While they may seem small, they will certainly lead to destruction.

- Fill out your time sheet accurately.
- Always work during work hours.
- If your work is complete, then help someone else.

- Never surf the internet or read Facebook during work hours.
- The owner is paying for your talent and time. Be faithful and be blessed.

If God leads you to start your own business, then be faithful to your customers. Be honest in all your dealings. Never, never, never take a bribe. Never pay a bribe. Both are wrong. The man who pays a bribe is no better than the one who asks for a bribe. Be an honest steward in all your dealings; then leave the results to the Owner of it all.

Do your best—always do your best! Study, be prepared, and then do your best. If you are truly prepared, then you will be able to leave, confidently, the rest in the hands of the Lord.

> **And which of you by worrying can add one cubit to his stature? If you then are not able to do the least, why are you anxious for the rest?**
>
> **—Luke 12:25-26**

God desires to be glorified by me and by you while we are on this earth. Do not let pride reign in your heart. God will reject you if you do. Humbly and faithfully serve the King with all your heart and He will lift you up.

> **Be clothed with humility, for God resists the proud, but gives grace to the humble.**
>
> **—1 Peter 5:5**

If you are full of yourself, God will not use you! God will not use the proud Christian. You have to rebuke your pride. God is not going to share His glory with anybody!

In order to deal with your pride, you must put your relationship with Him above everything else in your life. If you will, then and only then will He provide all the things that you need. It is at that point that He will begin to give you the desires of your heart. For, you see, His desires will become your desires. An amazing transformation takes place in your heart. As you seek Him, you want to do His will. It happens like turning a key to start the car.

The power of His Spirit will come upon you and you will become mighty in spirit—like the men of old. "Now to Him who is able to do immeasurably more than all we ask or imagine"—God is able to do so much that you cannot even measure what God is able to do.

Paul is saying in that Scripture that God is incredibly incredible, extravagantly extravagant, awesomely awesome in His awesomeness, outrageously outrageous, fantastically fantastic, amazingly amazing, infinitely infinite. Moreover, He is all of these, all of the time! If you can trust Him with your life, then you can trust Him with your finances.

> Consider the lilies, how they grow: they neither toil nor spin; and yet I say to you, even Solomon in all his glory was not arrayed like one of these.
>
> —Luke 12:27

> But seek the kingdom of God, and all these things shall be added to you.
>
> —Luke 12:31

Break out of the box—the common—the routine. Life in the box is not where God is! God is bigger than your box! God will not let you conveniently confine Him to your limits, your boundaries, your parameters. God wants out of the box and He wants you out of the box!

> Do not fear, little flock, for it is your Father's good pleasure to give you the kingdom.
>
> —Luke 12:32

No limits, no boundaries. Our God can do exceedingly more than we think or expect! Break out of the box, raise your limits, go beyond the boundaries.

God is able—there is power in Jesus Christ and in a relationship with Him. With God, you get more! You always get more with God. Our God is able to do far more abundantly beyond all we can ask. God exceeds the expectation. Trust Him. Always trust Him!

> Sell what you have and give alms; provide your-
> selves money bags which do not grow old, a treas-
> ure in the heavens that does not fail, where no thief
> approaches nor moth destroys. For where your
> treasure is, there your heart will be also.
>
> —Luke 12:33-34

You are to be faithful stewards of what God has placed into your hands. That means that you recognize that He owns it all and that you hold it with open hands.

If He asks you to give sacrificially, then do so with a glad heart! The Kingdom works that way. God gives to one so that He can bless another. In my life, I have found that God frequently gives one Believer surplus to supply a need in the life of another Believer. Why? It is because God wants to bless you more! His Word tells us that it is more blessed to give than to receive!

It is important to note that God blesses the heart attitude of the giver, not the gift itself.

God tells us to ask for what we need and that He will provide it. God will provide direction through the giving of funds. God will also provide direction through the withholding of funds. Just as you are ready to hear God's answer of a resounding yes, you must also be ready to hear Him when He says no.

Too many times, when God says no through the withholding of funds, Believers look for another way. They try to make a window where God has closed the door! They will go out and borrow money to buy what they want or to do what they want to do, then they will say things like, "I am trusting God to provide the monthly payment." No, a thousand times no! That is the world's way. Do not fall into that trap.

I will talk more about debt in the life of the Believer later, but first I must lay down some other principles.

Trusting God gives you that peace that passes all understanding.

> Therefore I say to you, whatever things you ask
> when you pray, believe that you receive them,
> and you will have them.
>
> —Mark 11:24

God wants to demonstrate trustworthiness in you. He wants you to demonstrate your trustworthiness to Him! It is not because God needs to see that you are a trustworthy steward; He already knows the end from the beginning.

We have the power to claim God's promises, but we must be willing to yield our rights to God—to obey, to serve Him. You have a right to claim what you need when you are serving Him with a whole heart. Now it is important to note that I am not speaking of a "name-it/claim-it" kind of Gospel. God promises to provide for our needs. He does not promise to give us our every whim.

If you are faithful, many times God will use you to meet the needs of others. This brings unity in the body of Christ. Do not make the mistake of trying to hold on to what is not yours.

Earn as much as you can without neglecting your other responsibilities. Give generously all the time. Give sacrificially, without hesitation, when the Lord leads you to do so. Save the rest. God frequently provides what we need ahead of time. Save for those unexpected circumstances that will certainly arise in your life.

The government has brought many opportunities into the life of our neighbors—like food stamps and welfare. The world has abused this concept in order to win votes. The people, including many Believers, have fallen into a trap.

The fact that the world has abused the concept of helping the needy does not mean that you should overlook it. Care about the needs of the widow and orphan, the saved and the unsaved, and God will bless you abundantly.

Ask yourself, "Where am I today financially? Where do I need to be in one year? Where do I need to be in ten years?" The answers to these three simple questions will give you the basis to developing a plan (budget) that will take you to the place that God is leading you. However, in order to do this you must become a man of vision.

A man with vision is a man who:

- Sees things before others see them.
- Sees what others do not see.
- Sees farther than others see.
- Sees the results before they happen.
- Sees his vision as his motivation.

Become a man of vision in your finances and you will begin to see the Lord bless in all areas of your life.

Chapter 4

Miracle at

Monte del Señor

by Alex Corzo

"We cannot but speak the things which we have seen and heard." That was the phrase Pastor Mike Richardson read when he visited us in June of 2015. Moreover, that was the very phrase that he used to launch an unbelievable challenge to our congregation, *Monte del Señor* (Mountain of the Lord) Church, which God has given me the honor of pastoring.

The initial challenge to buy the building that our church occupies in Mexico City was born almost three years ago. It is located in a working-class area that has very real problems of all kinds: family, financial, social, and of course, a tremendous need for God.

After a long struggle, we signed the purchase documents in December of 2012. The building we purchased is 53,800 sq. ft. It has multiple rooms and offices and a main auditorium that seats over 1,000 people. Many years ago, it had been a cinema showing all kinds of movies. Today, by God's grace, it is a center of worship where Jesus Christ is preached and God's people are edified. The building, including title registration fees, cost 15 million pesos. How did we ever manage to pay such an enormous amount of money, especially for a congregation of 700 people—most of them earning medium or low incomes?

Though our church had a savings fund set aside for the purchase of the building, it was insufficient for such a large purchase, so we developed a strategy to raise the financial resources necessary. A committee made up of me, as pastor, and my closest helpers, headed the plan, which consisted in obtaining a long-term loan from a bank. However, God, who sees all and knows what is best for us, did not allow it. All the doors we knocked on were closed. Banks, financial institutions, moneylenders and investors—nobody wanted to lend us the money!

On the eve of the purchase date, we had collected donations, the large majority of which were from our own congregation, to cover a little over 40% of the total cost. In order to cover the remaining amount, the Lord moved in the hearts of various church members to lend the church the remaining amount. Some lent from their savings and their investments. Some even borrowed money so that, when the date arrived, we had gathered in full the money required for the purchase. This was nothing compared to what God had prepared for us.

Up to this point, we had acquired a building for our church, but at the same time contracted a gigantic debt with some of our church members who had very kindly, with much love and trust, provided the necessary capital. It was imperative that we repay them with double honor and commitment. For this reason, we began to collect a special offering during every Sunday morning service, so that month after month we could make the payments to these brothers and sisters. That is what we did from January 2014 until June 2015, when we received a special visit from our friend, Pastor Mike Richardson.

I had met Brother Mike when I attended *"El Hogar Educador"* conferences in the city of Pachuca, Hidalgo. For several years my wife and I, as well as several members of our congregation, had been attending these conferences, due to the fact that we have been homeschooling our children. Given my interest in sharing this kind of teaching regarding our children's education, we contacted Pastor Mike and invited him to come visit us in order to give a series of talks to our church. He very kindly accepted. Maybe Pastor Mike thought, as I did, that he was merely going to visit another church (like so many that he had visited before) and give some messages (just as he has done in so many places for so many years). Nevertheless, neither he nor I could imagine what God had in store for our church on this occasion.

A few days before Brother Mike's arrival in Mexico City, I was called and informed that I needed to attend an event being held by our denomination's leadership (in Santiago Atitlán, in Guatemala) during the dates in which Pastor Mike would be visiting us. It was with great regret and sadness that I had to go and leave our guest to be looked after by our church without me being present. But this, too, happened as part of the work that God was about to carry out. Now, I see that if I had been with Pastor Mike, maybe I would have told him about the situation of our church regarding the debt that we still had to pay. Perhaps in some way I would have impeded the conscience of our Brother Mike, and as a result, the power that God was about to display.

That week Pastor Mike honored us in sharing God's Word with us. Friday and Saturday he gave a series of talks for families and parents, and then he concluded by preaching Sunday at our morning service. That same Sunday morning I was hurrying back from my trip to Guatemala, trying to make it in time to be with our invited speaker, if only at the end of the service. I remember arriving in a rush, near the end of the service; Pastor Mike had already concluded his message. I could sense in the air, and see on the faces of the congregation, that a beautiful ministry from God had taken place. I sat next to Mike and greeted him. Then I asked him how he was and if he had been treated well. I could not converse any more with him because the service was not over yet and I did not consider it very proper to continue talking any more at that time—there would be time to catch up with this servant of God later.

At that moment, a deacon went to the pulpit to collect the special offering allocated to the payments on the debt we had with our brothers and sisters who had lent the money for the purchase of our building. When the deacon took the microphone Mike asked me what this second offering was for, and I explained in a few words that it was for paying the debt on our building. It was at that moment that Mike did something totally unexpected and unprecedented. He asked me if he could say something to the congregation. Naturally, I did not have any problem with it; he was our guest and I knew he was there with a purpose. So Mike went up once again to the platform and asked for the microphone from the deacon who was about to collect the offering.

"We cannot but speak the things which we have seen and heard." Mike read aloud the words written behind him on the wall and continued. "That's a beautiful phrase, but we need to not only write it down—we need to live it." He said this in his characteristically calm demeanor. "Your pastor just explained to me what this offering is for, and I have asked his permission to do something. I'm afraid you all don't know me very well, but I'm a crazy gringo," he said jokingly. Then he asked, "How much is still owed on the building?" I quickly turned and asked the treasurer. We informed Mike that the amount of our debt was currently around four and a half million pesos. I thought I saw a hint of surprise on Mike's face as he humorously quipped, "Hmmm, that's about 300 cows! Yes, God can pay that off this very day. Those of you who were about to collect the offering, please return to your seats."

To be honest, I was worried. What was this "crazy gringo," as he had described himself, doing? I imagined what was coming next and part of me was stunned while the other part of me was becoming excited as I knew and had witnessed before the power of God.

"Today we will not be taking up an offering," Brother Mike continued his exhortation, "today we will pray for the supernatural provision of God to be manifested, because God doesn't want His people to be in debt. This debt that you have, due to the purchase of this building, will be paid this very week." How bold of him to say that!

Sometimes I think that not even Mike himself fully understood all that was going on; he was merely obeying the impulse of the Holy Spirit that counseled his heart.

Pastor Mike added, "God is going to pay off this debt with what you have. This week, each one of you should pray that the Holy Spirit would show you how much to give, and next week bring it to the Sunday morning service. With what you give to the Lord, you are going to pay off this debt. And do not forget that it is in sacrifice that you show your love for God and for His church." Ending with this exhortation, he said a prayer, put the matter in God's hands, and said goodbye.

What on earth is going to happen now? Lord Jesus, what are You going to do? How are You going to do it? These were the questions that went through my mind all of that week. To tell the truth, over more than 27 years as a Christian, I have seen many miracles and wonders of our God—but to pay off a debt of over four million pesos in one week? That I had never seen, and, frankly, I did not think my faith was quite that far reaching.

I continued this exercise in sincerity. I even went so far as to pray, "Lord, if what Brother Mike said was from You, help me to believe, and show me what I should do when such an amazing miracle occurs—if it occurs. But if it was only his own heart speaking, please show me how I should explain to the congregation why it did not happen."

The turmoil in my heart was so great that I did not preach at all during that week; instead, I devoted myself to prayer. I did not want to speak of the matter with the congregation since I felt in my heart that if I said something from the pulpit about the matter it might "tarnish" (for lack of a better term) what the Lord had left as a challenge to the congregation through our Brother Mike.

That week, two important things happened that I think are necessary to share, since they are a part of the way in which God worked to move His powerful hand in our lives. Halfway through the week, Pastor Mike got ahold of me and let me know that when he had arrived at his home in Arteaga, God had spoken to him, saying that, indeed, he had left a great challenge of faith at *Monte del Señor*, but how was he going to participate in this challenge? He let me know that he had determined to set aside an amount from his personal bank account in order to contribute to this cause. Sure enough, in accordance with his promise, before the week was out, Mike had transferred the funds to our church's account. This act overwhelmed me and was a both a great blessing and a great lesson, for Brother Mike had not only taught us with his words; he had gone further and taught us with his very actions and, in so doing, he had become a part of us.

This generous act moved my heart. My family and I were among the people to which the church owed money. For years, my wife and I had been saving to buy a house, but when the opportunity to buy a building for the church presented itself, we had given part of that amount as an offering and then we had contributed the rest of our savings as a loan. That week my wife and I talked about it and decided that we would give the part of our house savings, which the church owed us, as an offering and forgive that debt, and that is what we did. I did not know it or understand it, but the miracle was already starting.

Sunday arrived and I intentionally preached about a matter entirely unrelated to the offering that would be gathered to pay for our building. I did not want to, in even the smallest way, tarnish the words and ministry that Mike had left us with the week before. After I finished my message, I tersely told the congregation: "Well, Brothers and Sisters, the moment has come to do what Pastor Mike Richardson assigned us as a challenge of faith last week. I trust that during the week, each one of you has been praying and asking the Lord what it is that you should do. Now the moment has come to do it. Pastor Mike declared that today we would pay off the debt we have and now those who believe that, bring your offerings. And while we do that, let's spend some time praising the Lord." After I prayed, each member of the congregation came forward to place their offering in the collection plates that were at the altar. My heart trembled in expectation. I knew that if the miracle occurred at all, it would occur immediately, so I asked the congregation to remain and continue in praise while the financial team counted the offering. We waited to know what God had done.

After about 30 or 40 minutes, while the congregation sang and worshiped, I was called to a small room, next to the main auditorium, where a group of about eight people counted out the offering. When I entered, three of the women who were there were crying almost uncontrollably. Upon seeing them, I shuddered. This could only mean one of two things: either they were crying out of sadness and frustration because we had not met our goal, or they were crying because they were so moved that we had achieved our purpose. "What happened?" I asked. The church treasurer looked up and said with a very serious tone and manner, and in a broken voice, "It's been accomplished, Pastor; we do not have any debt anymore."

Even now, as I write this testimony, my heart weeps in gratitude. Never, ever, ever had I witnessed such a great wonder. I immediately left the room and went up once again onto the platform with the elders of the church. I stopped the singing, took the microphone, and once again addressed the congregation. I could barely speak; I had a knot in my throat and I could not keep back the tears. All I could do was to repeat the words of our treasurer. "Beloved saints, I want to tell you that it has been accomplished—our congregation has no more debt and this building is now completely ours and God's!"

The congregation broke out in great joy! We yelled, we cried, we jumped, and we danced! We remained for a good while singing, worshiping, and praising the great love of God and this recent demonstration of His mercy and power.

It is important to explain one more thing. When I again entered the room where the offering was being counted, I was given more details. God had done this miracle in two ways. The first was in moving the hearts of the congregation to make a sacrifice and give of their own resources to pay off this debt. The brothers and sisters of *Monte del Señor* Church did exactly that and they not only gave money; some gave jewels and watches, and in this way we raised close to 35% or 40% of the total.

The second part of the miracle occurred in this way: God moved some of the church members, whom we owed, to do the same as my wife and I had done. That is, to forgive the whole of the debt that we had with them, donating the total of the amount we owed them to this cause. In this way, what had occurred during the week was replicated in the congregation. In other words, Pastor Mike gave what was in his bank account as an offering. I agreed to cancel the part of the debt that was owed to me, and the members of the congregation did the same—they gave of their resources. Many decided to forgive what was owed them and, thus, spiritually expanded what we ministers had done first. This also shows us the importance of ministers' influence, even in what is done in private. Therefore, a chain reaction had occurred. An ever expanding and spiritual wave of blessing, faith, bravery, and love was divulged and spread among our congregation from the greatest to the least of the brethren.

The exact amount of our debt was 4,222,000 pesos. What was raised, between offerings in cash and canceling promissory notes, was close to 4,300,000 pesos. Some might say we actually raised more than what we owed, but since the challenge was to owe nothing, we also covered a debt we had contracted over repairs and adaptations that we had made to our building. We needed to settle the contractors and bricklayers' wages, as well as the cost of various construction materials. We were able to pay off that debt as well with the additional funds. That week the church was left without a single peso in the treasury but, thank God, completely debt free!

Ever since that visit from Pastor Mike to *Monte del Señor* Church, he and his family and his church became a part of us. We are not only united by the blood of Christ, but additionally this miracle from God has bonded us and linked us inextricably as Brothers, family, and friends.

Yes, Brother Mike definitely is a "crazy gringo," but he is also a transformed man of faith who, without realizing it, often causes the blessing of God that has covered him during his life and ministry, to spread in multiple ways along the path he walks. I can say with all freedom, because I've seen it, that Brother Mike knows what he is talking about when it comes to trusting God in the administration of your finances.

Today at *Monte del Señor* Church, we continue to proclaim more firmly than ever the words written in bold lettering behind our platform—the words that Pastor Mike Richardson, used by God, brandished so daringly, bringing us to a greater understanding of their meaning, "We cannot but speak the things which we have seen and heard."

Alex Corzo
Pastor, Monte del Señor
Mexico City

Chapter 5

Whom Do You Serve?

Spend less than you earn and do it for a long time. Then you will be financially stable and able to give generously. Earn as much as you can without neglecting your other responsibilities. Give generously all the time. Give sacrificially, without hesitation, when the Lord leads you to do so. Save the rest. God frequently provides what we need ahead of time. Save for those unexpected circumstances that will certainly arise in your life. These are four key points that you need to learn and make an integral part of your thought process. It is for that reason that I mention them again, here at the beginning of this section on servitude.

We, as Believers, are called to be servants of the King of kings, and it is precisely for that reason that Satan tries to shackle us and entangle us with financial bondage. For, you see, if we are entangled in financial problems our thoughts will focus on them instead of focusing on the God whom we serve.

Bound by Debt

It is important to note that debt is one of the symptoms of being in bondage. Therefore, the ultimate goal is not to simply pay off debt, but also to treat the underlying problem.

For example, many times young couples find themselves in debt because they are trying to build the lifestyle that their parents have and to do it in the first three years of marriage. This coveting attitude brings about the symptom of debt. Yes, we must treat the symptom—debt; we must also treat the problem—covetousness.

There are many common errors in judgment that tend to lead to debt.

- Get-rich-quick mentality
- Investing borrowed money
- Getting involved in things that you do not understand
- Ignoring your spouse's advice
- Not paying your debts

Allowing a get-rich-quick mentality to control your thinking and, ultimately, your decisions will lead to debt. This type of mindset is ultimately the result of covetousness and slothfulness. Instead of developing this outlook on life, work hard and be diligent.

Risking borrowed money to invest, or even to start a business is a danger that you should avoid. Trying to make money with other people's money is an age-old concept. Somehow, it seems easier to risk borrowed money. It is almost like finding money in the street. It does not seem real. Nevertheless, in the end, you must repay even if the business fails.

Getting involved in things that you do not understand is risky and foolish. If you do not understand it, how will you know if it is a wise investment? Study to show yourself approved. Read and learn. Obtain the knowledge needed before you invest money in anything.

Making financial decisions quickly leads to failure. Whether it is a salesman at your door or a business associate, if they are pushing to close a deal fast, it is usually because they know that what they are offering you is of little or no value. Do not become trapped in this type of snare. Always consider your steps carefully.

Ignoring your spouse's advice is devastating to your relationship and to your finances. Do not do it! While this principle generally applies to the husband more than the wife, both must be careful to follow it. If your spouse has a concern about a business investment or a purchase for the family, listen to the concern and consider your decision carefully. Do not be hasty in making a decision when your spouse expresses doubts. Peace in your home is the better option! In addition to that, most of the time, you will find out in the end that your spouse was right.

Trying to get out of paying debt that you have committed to in the past, whether through legal means, like bankruptcy, or by simply trying to hide from your debtors is wrong. Many family relationships have been broken because of unpaid loans taken from relatives. If you borrow, repay. Make the sacrifices necessary to have a good name. Your good name will ultimately be worth more than great riches! Even if the company writes off the debt as unrecoverable, do everything within your power to pay your debts.

Financial bondage is an attitude that robs you of your relationship with God or with your family. Physical bondage is one thing; mental bondage is another thing! Up until a few centuries ago, financial bondage meant just that—a physical bondage in debtor's prison!

> Agree with your adversary quickly, while you are on the way with him, lest your adversary deliver you to the judge, the judge hand you over to the officer, and you be thrown into prison. Assuredly, I say to you, you will by no means get out of there till you have paid the last penny.
>
> —Matthew 5:25-26

Today we no longer use physical bondage as a means of recovering an unpaid debt, but it has been replaced by something that is as bad or perhaps worse—mental bondage! Scripture is clear on this point: the borrower is servant to the lender!

> The rich rules over the poor, and the borrower is servant to the lender.
>
> —Proverbs 22:7

As a result of violating Scriptural principles, financial pressures mount up on families throughout the world, and the church is not exempt. These pressures are an important factor in the breakup of many marriages. Pressures and worries lead to a breakdown in communication, which leads to more arguments and fights, which, sadly, leads many into separation and divorce.

Contrary to what many believe, it is not just the lack of money that causes these problems. Many times, we worry about how to get more! Yet God clearly teaches us that we must learn to be content with what we have. On numerous occasions, you worry over keeping what you have—even when you have abundance. The underlying problem is always the same: attitude.

> Two things I request of You (Deprive me not before I die): Remove falsehood and lies far from me; Give me neither poverty nor riches—feed me with the food allotted to me; Lest I be full and deny You, and say, "Who is the LORD?" Or lest I be poor and steal, and profane the name of my God.
>
> —Proverbs 30:7-9

When dealing with poverty, the principle is clear: "Remove falsehood and lies far from me." Are you honest or are you dishonest?

When we begin to have abundance, it is not nearly as clear. In many cases, instead of being content with God, people become comfortable with His provision. The difference in those two may appear to be subtle, but in reality, they are great! Our contentment must be in God and God alone.

Know God's Plan for Your Life

In order to accept God's provision, you must first know God's plan for your life.

As I have mentioned, two people have dramatically affected my life and my understanding about finances. Larry Burkett, a man who taught powerfully about the topic of finances, and Daniel Thornton, a good friend and the one who introduced me to Larry's teaching. Daniel first encouraged me to get out of debt. I will be forever grateful for that encouragement. Had I not been debt free, I would have been unable to come to Mexico when invited. I have leaned heavily upon what I have learned from these two men.

Pam and I have had a heart for missions since we first accepted Christ. When missionaries or traveling evangelists would come to our church, we would always invite them to stay with us.

We had a desire to go to the mission field for years, but God had given us a vision for going without raising support ahead of time. The only way I could see that happening was to work hard and save enough money to support ourselves, then go to the mission field later in life. God had a different idea—to be completely dependent on Him and to trust Him for our needs!

After Pam and I attended a financial seminar taught by Daniel Thornton, the Lord began to deal with us about debt. We determined that it was His will for us to pay off all our debt and live the rest of our lives completely debt free. During the ensuing years, God provided us with many examples of how He meets every need of those who place their trust in Him.

It is important to note, God does not say that you cannot borrow money. Never borrow needlessly. Still, if you spend less than you earn and do it for a long time, you will be financially stable. It is easy to say this—spend less than you earn—but many times, it is hard to put it into practice. It will require sacrifice, it will require creativity, and it will require a consistent relationship with God and each other. Nevertheless, you can do it if you determine in your heart to live debt free.

Do You Trust God or Do You Just Say That You Trust God?

Shortly after attending Daniel's conference on finances, I accepted a job at a manufacturing company. It was the dream job for a young accountant. At twenty-eight years of age, I had become a Chief Financial Officer.

Pam and I had normal debt like most families have—house, car, and a few credit cards. By this time, we had developed a budget and a plan to get out of debt. Despite the new job, finances were tight due to the accelerated repayment plan we had set up for eliminating our debt.

After having worked just a few months, I received a bonus. I knew that it was the Lord's provision to help us in the process of debt reduction, but I wanted my kids to understand that as well. Instead of depositing the check into our bank account, I cashed the check and asked for all the money in ten-dollar bills.

That night after supper, I began to talk about our budget, finances, and debt. Then I told our children that the Lord had allowed me to receive a bonus. It was then that I began to pull out piles of ten-dollar bills from my pockets. With each stack, all the eyes around the table got bigger and bigger.

We counted it together—$4000.00. Then I told them about the debt that we could pay off with this money. In addition, since we would pay off the smaller loans, we could take the money we were paying on the smaller loans and use it to pay the next one off even faster. The timing of that bonus gave me a tremendous illustration to my children about God's faithfulness.

There have also been some naysayers along the way. One example was the VP of marketing where I worked. I was in his office late one evening discussing business. Since I was the CFO and he was the VP of marketing, we had many such conversations. This one, however, took an unusual twist. As we were discussing company finances, the conversation turned to personal finances. After I began to explain how God provides for all our needs, he burst out in laughter saying, "God doesn't provide for your needs, this company does!"

He was not a Believer, but it still made me sad that he did not understand that God was in control. Not long after that meeting, he left the company. I wonder if he has ever come to comprehend the principle that God is in control.

Two years later, my family drove across the United States to attend a conference in Oklahoma. Throughout the week, we were excited and encouraged. As we drove out of the parking lot on the final day, I was surprised by a loud bang which was followed by a sickening thud and then finally nothing—nothing but dead silence. The hours that followed once again provided a living example of a loving God that meets every one of our needs.

Skip Purcell, a local Believer, helped me find a mechanic to replace the engine. He, along with his wife Mary, offered to let us stay in their home while the mechanic repaired the car. The conference organizer paid me to fly home so that I could return to work on time. A week later Skip checked out the car and Pam drove home.

Despite God's provision in the midst of troubling circumstances, I could not understand why God would allow this to happen since we were committed to getting out of debt. Over seven years later, I finally understood why God allowed this to happen at that time in our life.

God used many circumstances during those years to purify our hearts and lives. God was using them to prepare us for the mission field.

We first met a man from Monterrey in July of 1993. He told us about the ministry of his local church. The next day he asked us to consider coming to Mexico to help their church. After praying about it, we drove down and met with the pastor and the elders. While we were visiting, we agreed, as a family, that God was calling us to Mexico. We moved there fifteen days after our visit in August 1993.

I finally understood why God had allowed that car to break down so many years earlier. For, you see, it was Skip Purcell who introduced us to his friend from Monterrey. I did not understand that at the time, but now I do. He used those car problems for our good. He used those circumstances, as well as Skip and Mary, to open the door for us to go to Mexico!

Even when we do not understand, God is working in our lives to bring about His will. Do not rebel in times of trouble! God is working all things together for your good. You can count on that! Trust God even when you do not understand!

Upon returning to Georgia after our visit to the church in Monterrey, we began to prepare for the move. I gave my accounting client list to a friend and wrote a letter to my clients advising them that we were moving to Mexico. After selling or giving away most of the furnishings in our home, we took a small trailer of belongings with us. We turned our house over to the real estate agent that was going to manage it for us. He had it rented within one week.

During our first years in Mexico, the offerings from the church in Mexico, the rent we received for our house, and our personal savings met our personal needs and the ministry expenses.

It was the Mexican church *Vida Nueva* and its members whom God used to sow a deep and profound love for Mexico and its people in our hearts. We will always be grateful to them for the love that they have shown us throughout the years.

Though we never sought financial support, the Lord began to bring in the income required to continue the work here in Mexico. Each year, as the work expands, the Lord is faithful to meet all of our needs, both personal and ministry-related. We have learned that God knows our needs even before we do and that He is faithful in providing for them. It is often through the giving or withholding of finances that He gives us final direction.

I must tell you that several times I have been tempted to place my trust in people rather than in the Lord. Nevertheless, He has shown me repeatedly that my calling is to become completely dependent on Him. If I will seek Him and His righteousness, He will supply my need from His abundance.

We are serving our Lord here in Mexico simply because we feel He has called us to this country and to the Spanish-speaking people of the world for a lifetime. When God calls you to do something, He provides the resources needed and the way to do it. That does not mean that it will always be easy. Sometimes it is tough. But once you have made your calling sure, rest in it and trust in the Lord for His provision.

> For the gifts and the calling of God are irrevocable.
>
> —Romans 11:29

It was over thirty years ago that Pam and I made the decision to get out of debt in order to be able to dedicate our lives to serving God. Today, we still maintain the same conviction—living debt free.

Debt Limits Our Service to God

Success in ministry or success in life will not be measured by the big things—the magazines we published, the conferences where I speak, our evangelism efforts. Real success is measured by the lasting impact that we have on our family.

Acts chapter nine tells how Paul met the Lord on the road to Damascus. In verse nine, he asked the Lord, "What will you have me to do?" From that day forward, he followed Christ in all aspects of his life. His needs were met, not because he had a great abundance, but because he learned how to be content. He told Timothy to be content with food and clothing.

> And having food and clothing, with these we shall be content.
>
> —1 Timothy 6:8

In order to become ever more effective in our quest to follow God and do His will, I believe that this verse must be applied in our lives. However, most of us are almost never satisfied with just our basic needs. We have many wants and desires—many things that we really do not need. Many people are in debt trying to fulfill their wants and desires—things they cannot afford. Yet 1 Timothy 6:6 says, "Godliness with contentment is great gain!"

Ask yourself the same question that I asked myself nearly three decades ago, "Do I trust God, or do I just say that I trust God?" If you answered that you trust God, then ask yourself one more question. Your answer will reveal your true heart attitude. Will you cut up your credit cards the first time that you do not pay them off in full at the end of the month?

Our prayer must be, "God, help me to know Your Word and apply it in my life. Help me to be content with the circumstances in my life, with where You have called me, and with what You have given me." God not only wants us to live by faith but also to live a life that demonstrates contentment. Godliness with contentment is great gain!

God wants Believers to have an eternal perspective. This earth is not our home. We are strangers and pilgrims in this land. We must keep our eyes focused on our home—heaven. We don't live on this earth in order to have a life of ease. We live here to serve God with our whole heart—to do His will.

At times God's will requires us to sacrifice our wants and desires. At times God may even call us to give up physical benefits (like houses, cars, or even money) in order to gain spiritual blessings. True success is finding the will of God and doing it. When we give to God, He always returns much more than we give. However, it is important to understand that, most of the time, He gives us something of far greater value—spiritual blessings!

We are not here to entertain ourselves, to accumulate a fortune and die. We are here to do the will of the Father! We are here to serve Him faithfully! We must not, we cannot, allow ourselves to be distracted by our wants and our desires—materialism.

> Lay not up for yourselves treasures upon earth, where moth and rust doth corrupt, and where thieves break through and steal: But lay up for yourselves treasures in heaven, where neither moth nor rust doth corrupt, and where thieves do not break through nor steal: For where your treasure is, there will your heart be also.
>
> —Matthew 6:19-21

Larry Burkett defines debt as bondage. He goes on to say, "Money borrowed and repaid according to the agreement is not debt, but an obligation." He adds, "Bondage [debt] can also occur if other biblical principles are violated."

It is true that debt is an obligation to pay, but I believe that it is much more than that. Debt is not sin, but it is a limiting factor in our life.

Be a Very Careful Borrower!

Debt works against you instead of for you. Compound interest is working for the lender and putting the borrower in more and more bondage. For example, if you borrow $100,000 to buy land so that you can build a house and finance that land for 30 years at 10% interest, you will pay back a total of $315, 925!

In many ways, debt is like a trap for animals. It is very easy to get into but very hard to get out. The world makes it sound so tempting. "Buy now, no payments for three months." When that fourth month comes, the glamor has worn off, but the bills need to be paid. It is easy to float down a river—going with the current, but when you try to paddle a kayak upstream, it takes a tremendous amount of strength and effort. Getting into and out of debt is the same.

Surety is very similar to debts and obligations, yet there are subtle differences. It is of utmost importance that you take the time to understand the differences—otherwise you will fall into the snare.

There are two forms of surety. Cosigning is the most widely known form of surety. Do not ever cosign! If the bank or lending institution does not trust someone to repay, why should you? If there is a need in that person's life, God might lead you to help meet that need through the giving of a gift, but do not cosign!

Sometimes adult children put pressure on their parents to cosign. Do not cosign for them. Never ask someone to cosign for you either. The Bible is clear on this topic.

> My son, if you become surety for your friend, if
> you have shaken hands in pledge for a stranger,
> you are snared by the words of your mouth; you
> are taken by the words of your mouth. So do this,
> my son, and deliver yourself; for you have come

into the hand of your friend: Go and humble yourself; plead with your friend.

—Proverbs 6:1-3

He who is surety for a stranger will suffer, but one
who hates being surety is secure.

—Proverbs 11:15

A man devoid of understanding shakes hands in a
pledge, and becomes surety for his friend.

—Proverbs 17:18

The second form of surety is when you have no sure way
(guaranteed) to repay. The Bible tells us in Proverbs 22:7 that "The
rich rules over the poor, And the borrower is servant to the lender."

It is important to note that a job does not provide a sure
(guaranteed) way to repay. Owning your own business does not
provide a sure (guaranteed) way to repay. You could lose your job
or your largest customer could go out of business. Having enough
money in savings does not provide surety—a sure (guaranteed)
way to pay. The bank could make poor investments and end up
closing down, or the money you have invested in stocks could be
lost due to the company going bankrupt.

The only way that you can avoid surety is if the item for which
you borrow will stand for 100% of the liability that you owe on it.

Let me give you an example of avoiding surety. Let us assume
that you need a new stove. You go down to the store to buy one but
only have $100 in savings. You find a stove that you believe will
meet your needs but it costs $500. The store agrees to let you take it
home with a 20% down payment and you agree to pay the rest in
payments.

Does that debt create an obligation, or is it surety (the lack of a
guaranteed way to pay the debt)? If the day comes that you cannot
pay the monthly payment and the store will accept the return of the
stove as payment in full, then it is a debt—an obligation. However,
if your lack of payment allows the store to sue you for the balance
owed, rather than just taking back the stove, then it is surety. I
seriously doubt that many banks or lenders would ever take back

the now used stove. If they will not, the loan is surety because you have no guaranteed way to pay. Avoid surety. Run from it. Do not get into surety!

Borrowing presumes on the future, denies God the opportunity to show Himself strong in your life, destroys the opportunity to build your faith, and halts the opportunity to let your life be a living example to those around you. Both forms of surety are the most commonly violated financial principles in the Bible. Do not do it!

In the New Testament we are taught in Matthew 6:24 that, "No one can serve two masters; for either he will hate the one and love the other, or else he will be loyal to the one and despise the other. You cannot serve God and mammon."

While it is true that a man who carries debt can serve God, his ability to serve God is limited. When we have debt, we are limited in our ability to serve God because we must "serve" the lender. We must work for the lender. We must repay him. When the righteous borrow, they repay!

When you do not have debt, you have a greater freedom to go where God calls you, to give when God asks you to do so, and a greater ability to work for the advancement of the Gospel.

When someone borrows to make a purchase, he has lacked the self-discipline to save for the item or the self-control to deny himself the item. When someone is in debt, it is usually related to wrong attitudes.

Let us think about Christmas. How many families spend more than they should or even go into debt during that time of year just to buy presents for their children? Is that something that would bring glory to Jesus, the One whose birth you are celebrating?

And He said to them, "Take heed and beware of covetousness, for one's life does not consist in the abundance of the things he possesses."

—Luke 12:15

It is important to mention here that you are not to judge others who have debt. You can teach them, you can help them, but you must never judge them. Most of the time, one is in debt not because of the lack of faith, but because of the lack of prior teaching.

Is it reasonable to avoid debt in our society? Is it logical to save and then buy, or is it rational to buy now and pay later?

These are questions that you must answer but perhaps a better question would be, "What does the Bible tell us on this topic?"

> Offer to God thanksgiving, and pay your vows to the Most High. Call upon Me in the day of trouble; I will deliver you, and you shall glorify Me."
>
> —Psalms 50:14-15

God Always Looks at the Attitude of the Heart

It is important to note that bondage can also exist with the abundance of money—hoarding, stinginess, lack of generosity. God must always be our confidence! God does not condemn wealth; He condemns the misuse of wealth. Our attitude is the key factor. It is not what you do; it is why you do it.

> For what profit is it to a man if he gains the whole world, and is himself destroyed or lost?
>
> —Luke 9:25

Frustration, fear, and anxiety are typically associated with debt-related problems. Worry is not the problem. It is an outside indicator of the lack of trust in God.

Things to avoid:

- Problems arise from laziness, deceitfulness, greediness, and covetousness. Laziness is the lack of desire to be excellent.
- Slothfulness is the lack of desire to do what we know we need to do. Hunger is good if it makes a sluggard go to work.
- You must bring your indulgences under control. Indulgence is buying something that you do not really need.
- Do not let material things take precedence over your relationship with God or your family.
- Do not risk money that you cannot afford to lose.
- Greediness is the desire to have more than you have.
- You must also be careful with over commitment to work. It will affect you and your family. Many elevate

overwork today. Many times that type of person will get the promotion. They will "get ahead" but eventually they will likely lose it all. If you are not available to win others for Christ, you have a big problem in your life. Deal with it now! Do not wait.

Is it better to be a rich Christian or a poor Christian? What do you think? You can do more with more. Nevertheless, God wants you to be content with what you have!

> It is vain for you to rise up early, to sit up late, to eat the bread of sorrows; For so He gives His beloved sleep.
>
> —Psalm 127:2

1 Timothy 6:17-18 tells us clearly what God's attitude toward wealth is.

> Command those who are rich in this present age not to be haughty, nor to trust in uncertain riches but in the living God, who gives us richly all things to enjoy. Let them do good, that they be rich in good works, ready to give, willing to share.
>
> —1 Timothy 6:17-18

The Solution

Now that we have covered the topic of debt, as well as the reasons to avoid it, I believe that it is important to talk about the solution if you find yourself in debt. If you find yourself in that position, you, like me, can gain freedom from that bondage.

You must first transfer ownership to God. As you learned earlier, He is already the owner of it all. You must work toward getting out of debt. It is possible, and it will bring great freedom in your life.

Transferring ownership to God may seem like an easy thing to do. Write down on a piece of paper, "God, I deed everything to you." Without a doubt, God will test you on it—perhaps the next morning! Transferring ownership is a hard emotional process. It is not easy, but you must do it. God said to delight yourself in Him, and not in the things that you own.

There was a time that this was put to the test in my life. Pam and I had agreed to purchase two tracts of land, over 250 acres, for the Family Camp and for a radio tower to reach the surrounding area with the Gospel.

The owner and I agreed to the purchase price. It was a fair price. He understood that I would buy it only if I had the money in hand to do so. He understood my conviction about debt.

Nearly ten months passed and I still did not have the money. It was with great sorrow that Pam and I returned to his house and told him that we did not have the money to buy the property. He immediately offered to let me buy it and make payments. I refused. When we walked out of his house Pam said, "I am relieved that this is over with. We do not have to think about it anymore."

Those were not my feelings. My heart was tearing apart. I did not understand. This was a dream that I was certain that God had given me. For nine years, I had waited and negotiated for this property. We had agreed to a price that we both thought was fair. Despite all of this, God did not provide the funds to purchase the property. If I really believed what God had shown me back in 1986, that I was to live debt free the rest of my life, I had no choice but to walk away from the purchase, and I really did believe that!

I walked away, but I was heartbroken. Not because of the land, but because I had thought for nine years that this was the Lord's will in my life. That tore me up on the inside. How could I have been so wrong?

A few weeks later, I was visiting my friend Daniel Thornton. I told him about the property. He looked at me and said, "I still believe that it is God's will." Then he prayed and asked God to provide the funds.

Once you have made a decision to get out and stay out of debt, Satan will tempt you in many ways—trying to get you to go back into bondage. Do not do it! Instead, go to the Lord in prayer. Ask Him to show you His will and to give you direction.

If you are currently in debt, you must get out of debt. Start where you can. If you do not make a plan to get debt free, you will never get there. Create a vision for your life.

Begin to save regularly—something out of every paycheck. If you do not set aside something regularly, eventually a crisis will happen and it will tend to lead to debt. If you begin to save regularly, you will build up a reserve that will take care of those crises. This goes back to the principle of spending less than you earn.

Excel at what you do. If you do not have the knowledge you need, go and find someone who does and ask him. Evaluate your purchases before buying!

- Does the purchase help you better serve God?
- Is it really a necessity or do I just "really want it"?
- Do I need it? Can I live without it?
- Is this the best buy? Can I search around and get a better deal?
- Does it build up your family or will it tear it down?
- What are the maintenance costs?
- Will its value quickly go down?

Once you answer these questions then you will be prepared to determine if you should buy it, when you have the cash to do so.

Begin to use a written budget.

> **A man's heart plans his way, but the LORD directs his steps.**
>
> **—Proverbs 16:9**

Buy on a cash-only basis. If you do not have the funds to make a purchase, save for it. If you do not borrow money, you cannot get into debt. If you do not borrow more money, you cannot get into more debt. I can testify to you that it is the most freeing thing that you will ever do!

Accept God's direction. His wisdom will lead you and guide you. Turn to His Word and He will teach you.

> **Therefore do not worry, saying, 'What shall we eat?' or 'What shall we drink?' or 'What shall we wear?'**
>
> **—Matthew 6:31**

Make your decisions cautiously and carefully. The hand of the diligent will lead to plenty. Work hard and excel in what you do.

Do not be slothful. Set excellence as the minimum acceptable standard.

Confess your past wrong deeds and make them right. That is restitution! If you have stolen from your employer, go back and confess your sin, and then make restitution. God will bless you for it.

Let me tell you about a situation that happened shortly after I committed my life to Christ.

I was working in the day as a painting contractor and going to school at night. I was studying accounting. Pam and I already had three children. Work was slow in the construction industry so I began looking for another type of employment. Since I only lacked one year to finish my degree, I thought that finding a job in accounting would be beneficial in the long run.

One day, as I was driving through Lawrenceville, Georgia, I saw an employment agency and decided to stop. After speaking with the interviewer for a while, he made a phone call and then gave me the address for Johnson, Frazier and Wright, CPA.

I was excited to be going to an interview with a CPA firm. It astonished me when they offered me the job during my first interview. The owners were Believers. They trusted me from the very beginning, just as they trusted all of their employees. I was obviously in an entry-level position. My salary was fair for the work that I was doing. Finances were tight for a family of five living on an entry-level salary, but living frugally, we were able to pay the bills. This was in the USA where most people paid their bills with a check by mail, unlike today, where bills are paid electronically.

There was a postage machine in the office and all employees used it. Beside the machine, there was a cup where we would put the money for the postage that we had used. It is with deep regret, remorse, and shame that I tell you this story.

One day I had some bills to pay, but did not have any money in my pocket. I posted the letters and put them in the mail. I had full intentions to put the money in later—at least I thought I did. It was such a little thing—less than one dollar. No one even noticed that I had not put the money in the cup.

The next time that I went to pay the bills, I felt God prompting my heart. Pay for the last letter too! I pushed it down. I justified it; they have a lot of money and I only make a little. They will not miss it. I deserve it. I work hard.

I wish I had listened to the voice of God's Spirit, but I did not. As the months passed, it became easier and easier to "forget" to put the money in the cup.

Compromise is that way—it gets easier with each small step. After graduating from college, I was offered another job from another firm. I put the "little compromises" that I had made behind me. I did not want to think about them anymore.

One day, years later, God brought that back to my memory. I cried, "Oh God, how can I go back and tell them what I did?" I did not even know how much money it had been. I was sure that it was not much more than twenty dollars. Without a doubt, it did not exceed thirty dollars. "God, it doesn't make sense to drive all the way across Atlanta to talk about such a little thing."

The conviction continued to grow in my heart. I had to do it. I had to humble myself in order to go and talk with them. I gave them one hundred dollars to make sure that I was covering the money I had taken, plus all the interest. It was hard, but it was right. A burden lifted from my spirit. I had made restitution and God blessed me for it.

Maybe you have cheated an employer or a business associate. Perhaps you have cheated when reporting your income for tax purposes. It is even possible that some have never reported their income for tax purposes.

The first step is to confess your sin to God. The next is to stop sinning! After that go and confess your lies and deceit to those whom you have wronged. Then make restitution.

There may be consequences for what you did, but in spite of the consequences, God will bless you with abundant spiritual blessings—a closer relationship with Him.

With the power of the Spirit of God, learn to overcome greediness, covetousness, and discontentment. Live a moderate lifestyle. Do what it takes to live frugally. Put things back into balance.

Provide for the needs of your family. Do not sacrifice their needs to make more money. Be content.

Learn to sacrifice your desires to meet needs in your family and to be able to give generously to others who are in need. Put others before yourself. Do not be haughty. Do not ever think that you are better than someone else is. Give, and you will be blessed more than those who receive.

Freedom is the absence of bondage. Financial freedom is being released from financial bondage.

Chapter 6

What Do You Do?

Suddenly a situation becomes problematic and you are asked for a bribe.

What do you do?

For example, you may or may not have been violating the law when you were stopped, but you know what is going to happen. We have all been there and done that! Paying a bribe may seem like the easy way out of a traffic ticket. However, the reality is that bribery is contributing to widespread corruption. If you are asked for a bribe, it is your duty to refuse to pay it.

Bribery, extortion, corruption, ransom payments, and now even express kidnappings are rampant in Mexico. What should you do? How do you handle these types of situations? These are very important questions.

Christ gave His life to redeem sinners. That redemption will bring about a change in the lives of those who believe and will ultimately bear the fruit of righteousness. The Believer's goal is to reflect Christ in every action. Therefore, as Believers, we must avoid even the appearance of evil. That would certainly, and without a doubt, include all forms of corruption and bribery—including what many call "tipping" in Mexico.

Sadly, bribery has become a stumbling block for many Believers. It happens repeatedly. What do you do? Bribery, extortion, corruption, ransom payments, and express kidnapping payments are a vicious cycle. When people pay, the lawbreaker is encouraged to do it again. When I tell people that it should be reported they say, "The police are corrupt; if we report it, the situation will become worse." Ponder this for a moment.

Asking for a bribe is illegal; paying a bribe is illegal. Kidnapping is illegal; paying ransom money is frowned upon by law enforcement. Do we not serve a God who is big enough to work through these types of situations without violating the law?

> Surely oppression destroys a wise man's reason,
> and a bribe debases the heart.
>
> —Ecclesiastes 7:7

The ultimate question that needs answering is, "How should one respond to a request for a bribe?"

> Did I ever say, "Bring something to me"? Or, "Offer a bribe for me from your wealth"?
>
> —Job 6:22

> A wicked man accepts a bribe behind the back to pervert the ways of justice.
>
> —Proverbs 17:23

Unfortunately, most people wait until they are faced with the decision to even consider the implications. Then, because of the pressure, a bribe is paid and a routine is set in their lives. Once paid the first time, the conscience starts to become seared, and the mental justification begins. By the third or fourth time, it is second nature—just something that everyone does—and it is what you must do to live in this country. Nevertheless, the truth is that he simply went to the fight without preparing. He was weak-willed. He was unwilling to stand for his convictions. All of this was likely due to lack of preparation—in both the ways of honest business practices and the ways of God.

While many try to justify bribery as the custom here in Mexico, the mere fact that they would never announce publicly that they paid a bribe demonstrates that they themselves know that what they did was wrong. Some will say that they did it for the greater good; in other words, that the "end justifies the means." That is simply wrong.

In the late 1990s our magazine began growing dramatically so we decided to print it ourselves. We made a quick trip to Virginia to pick up a printing press and other equipment.

When we were bringing the equipment into Mexico, we had a five-hour border adventure. Since you are supposed to pay import taxes on things brought into Mexico, I pulled into the declaration line. I told the officer the equipment value. He told me that I would have to go through a customs broker. He gave me directions to the broker's office then added, "You can leave your car here while you work on getting the proper paperwork.

At the office, we agreed on a price for the broker's services. He said that it would take a couple of hours to finish the paperwork. The kids and I went to a little taco stand on the side of the street and ate lunch.

When I returned to the office, the broker told me that my documents were at the office for small importations—importation of less than $1,000. I knew that office was not the correct place to pay my taxes, since my equipment was worth more than $1,000.

When I returned to the importation office, I saw one of my invoices even though a clerk was trying to keep me from seeing it. The amount had been reduced!

I questioned the correctness of paying my taxes at that office but the clerk kept assuring me that this was the correct way to handle our import. I knew that the broker was trying to cheat the government by paying a smaller amount of taxes and keeping the difference, but I did not know what I could do about it.

When the clerk asked for the money, it was the amount I had agreed on at the first office. When I asked if the clerk was going to give me an official receipt for all the money, he assured me that he would. I did not know what to do.

I paid the money then bowed my head and prayed. "Lord, if this transaction is not correct, work it out. Bring justice."

As we walked out the door, the first officer I had spoken to walked up. He asked the clerk, "What's he doing here? His load is too big for a small importation." The fellow was very nervous and started trying to make up excuses. The first officer that I had spoken with turned out to be the head of the government's importation office. He grabbed the papers out of the clerk's hand and said he was going to talk to the customs broker that he had sent me to see.

The department head and the customs broker went into the main office. Later, he called me into the meeting. He also called for the customs broker to come to the meeting. The department head questioned both of us. Then he sent both of us out of the room.

Later, the customs broker was called back in the room. When they came out of the office, the department head told me that the customs broker was going to correct my paperwork. Later, in his office, the customs broker was mad for being caught. He left and told the department head that I had canceled the process and was going back to the United States!

A few minutes later, the department head asked me if I had canceled the paperwork. When I told him no, he left again and went back to the main building. Upon his return, he told me that he had received special permission to handle the importation without using a customs broker since I had been there for so long. Within thirty minutes, my documents were finished and I was ready to leave.

As I was preparing to leave, I went over to the department head to thank him for his help. He told me that he had called ahead to the checkpoint and told them that I was coming through and that they were not to give me any hassle. As I was leaving, he pointed to the government office that had been involved in the deception. All the lights were off and no one was there. He said, "We closed that office and sent everyone home."

It was worth the five-hour delay to see an honest official stand up and carry out justice!

You must understand that it does not always turn out this way. At times, the cost of not complying with a bribe request can be great. The Believer must be willing to "pay the price" to do what is right. That is just as true with bribery as it is in every other aspect of our lives as Believers. One may pay a high price by not submitting to the bribe, but God is glorified and that is our ultimate goal.

Steven Falkiner is a Believer who has set a high standard for others to follow. As a missionary, he paid a high price for his Biblically-based convictions. He, his wife, and their two daughters returned from Nepal in 1997 after failing to get long-term visas as missionaries, due to his refusal to pay bribes. I am grateful for his testimony and his teaching. It has helped many Believers to better understand this important issue. My ability to clearly express my thoughts and my writings on this issue have been influenced greatly by his teaching.

Bribery hinders development, denies justice, and oppresses the poor. When a bribe is paid, the one who pays is no less guilty of perverting justice than the one who receives the bribe. Paying or receiving a bribe is not and never will be the right option for a true Believer in Jesus Christ. As Believers, we should be, we must be, involved in the political process—without contaminating ourselves with bribery. We must befriend those in power. We are the hands and feet of Jesus here on this earth. We must be involved. We must be informed. We must be honest. Nevertheless, as foreigners, our impact will not be on Election Day. Our impact will be in the day-in, day-out life of the public officials whom we attempt to serve for Jesus.

> **For here we have no continuing city, but we seek
> the one to come.**
>
> **—Hebrews 13:14**

The quickest way to gain and maintain influence in the political arena is to do what others will never do. It is simple. It is easy — well, at least it is easy to propose. One must be absolutely committed to follow through. Otherwise, Christ's image is tarnished in the eyes of the politician.

It is the same in every country. People seek and search out the politician because they need or want something from the politician or government official. Yet, as Believers, we are called to serve. Therefore, I believe that we should seek out the politician and ask questions like, "How can I help you?" or "What can I do for you?" Think about it. It is really a simple yet profound concept—seeking to serve those whom we call "public servants." I believe it is a unique concept, its basis is in the very foundations of Scripture. The Believer can and should serve others for the advancement of the Kingdom.

There is, I believe, a problem in the lives of many people that prevents them from carrying out this simple practice of "serving the servant" and, thereby, being an effective witness for Jesus

Christ. That problem is a lack of spiritual life and growth in the Believer. Our society, our schools, and even our parents have drilled into our heads from a very early age that success equals money. So the underlying problem is our love of money—our desire to get rich—our desire to show how important we are by having things. Yet God calls Believers to be different. God calls us to be not just willing to give up everything for the Gospel; he actually calls us to do so. Few have ever done that, few ever will. Yet Jesus Christ, our supreme example, did so. He gave up heaven and all its riches to come and live among men so that we could have life and have it more abundantly!

Can you not give up some of the comforts of this world to serve those around you? Can you not risk financial loss in order to maintain standards of honesty in dealing with officials, and then turn around and risk even greater loss by offering, and really meaning it, to serve them—to help them? Yet our desire to get rich and amass even greater wealth not only prevents us from doing this, it actually causes many of us to do the exact opposite.

God ties living a successful life to knowing Him, meditating on His Word, and doing His will. God revealed Himself through His Word. It is only through the study and application of it that we will really come to know Him in an intimate way. Most people have no concept of the awesome privilege that we have received—to literally know and walk with God, the One who not only created the earth but also created you and me.

We must not squander our lives on fleeting and passing things, and as a result, fail to know God as an intimate friend. God, who possesses every bit of knowledge and wisdom there is, has explained the best way to live and, thus, how to keep you from squandering your life.

I encourage you to go against the flow. It will require strength and courage. You are called to be Christ-like in your attitudes, your actions, and even your thoughts. Go in a different direction and pursue different goals. Your passion must be for Christ and the truth of His Word.

Bribery, extortion, and protection money may be the norm for others, but you must stand out from the crowd. You must be different. You, as a Believer, must not simply sit on the sidelines watching life pass you by. You must not hold anything back. You must give it your all. You must fight the good fight. You must be faithful in your service for the King of kings and the Lord of lords.

In other words, you must learn to judge all things only by the price they shall gain in eternity.

An Impossible Dream Comes True!

During the time that I was reaching out to a war-torn area in northern Mexico, I wrote: "It was early November 2010, when the Lord began giving me a special burden for Ciudad Mier."

Since that time, I have made many trips in and through the area. During these trips, I have met Believers, government officials, military, and others. During my first trips into the town, I began to formulate a plan to hold a citywide evangelistic meeting. I wrote and printed a booklet for the soldiers and people living in this area about overcoming bitterness and about salvation. Despite my initial excitement, there were roadblocks at every turn. It seemed that the idea of doing anything other than one-on-one personal evangelism just was not an option.

The reasons were many. I was told, "People will not come out for a large public meeting. It is too dangerous. They will not answer their doors for strangers. It is too risky to take a group of Christians into the area. The times are too uncertain. Everyone is afraid."

I finally decided that the only option I had was to postpone the outreach campaign and continue to focus on the military, government officials, and individuals that I met along the way. During the last five months, I have been able to speak to many individuals about the Lord, but there have been few chances to reach the masses.

The truth is that, throughout the years we have lived in Mexico, our ministry has always focused primarily on the individuals and families—not the masses. This idea—this plan—for Mier was a different way of thinking for me.

This year my son and I planted a large plot of corn. When we were planting, I was not thinking about the hundreds—perhaps thousands—of ears of corn that we might harvest. I was thinking about the wonderful flavor of a single ear of sweet corn.

In the same way, our style of ministry has always been to touch individuals or families for Jesus. It is true that over the years the Lord has allowed us to reach more than just a few, especially with the ministry of *El Hogar Educador*. Nevertheless, it is important to understand that even in that aspect of our ministry, the motivating factor was always to reach individual fathers and their families. If many are reached, it is simply the result of adding up the individuals, because they are the focus.

So going back to an approach which involved reaching individuals in Mier was very comfortable and natural for me. Yet, there was still that feeling, deep inside me, that we needed to do more. It was like the cornfield. I was thinking about that one ear of sweet corn—yet we planted thousands of seeds. In much the same way, I felt like we needed to get many seeds sown in Mier without losing sight of that one precious soul who might come to know the Lord.

Until two weeks ago, every time I spoke to Presidente Alberto Gonzalez Peña about the needs in Ciudad Mier he would ask that we pray for him and the city. He never expressed any other physical needs. Sixteen days ago, when he told me, "If you and the brothers could help with this need," that he would be grateful, I wrote, "I have been asking the Lord for an open door in this city and I believe that the Lord has just swung the door wide open and He used four simple words: 'How can I help?'"

In hindsight, especially considering the events of the last two days, I think that I really understated and underestimated what the Lord was beginning to do in Ciudad Mier! I met with Alberto, his wife, and five of his staff members for several hours yesterday. I now have a clearer picture of some of the struggles and hardships in the area.

Previously, the Presidente had asked me if the brothers could help provide some food for one hundred families. However, due to the problems in the area, including a decrease in the number of available jobs, the mayor's staff is actually trying to help approximately 500 families.

Within that number, around 50 elderly and disabled people have no significant help available locally. The mayor's staff has set up a "Meals on Wheels"-type program and is providing them with hot meals on a daily basis. Additionally, there are not five or six, but many (I do not have the exact number yet) folks with unmet medical needs.

We were planning to provide at least five wheelchairs, walkers, and food that would meet 100 families' needs for a week. Once I realized that the need was much greater than I had imagined, I prayed silently and asked the Lord what our involvement should include. When I began to tell Don Alberto that we would try to provide basic food packages for five hundred families by next week, I must admit that I was committing to stretch our available resources to a point that I did not fully understand. I committed to doing everything possible to provide 2000 pounds of canned corn, 2000 pounds of canned vegetables, 1000 pounds of dried beans, 1000 pounds of rice, 1100 pounds of corn flour, 1100 pounds of wheat flour, 550 pounds of pasta, 2000 cans of tuna, and 500 liters of vegetable oil. All of this was in addition to the wheelchairs and walkers. While we had already acquired part of this at the time of the meeting, I did not even know the current cost of many of the products!

After talking about it for a while, we decided that the best way to make sure that these resources were placed into the hands of the people who needed them the most was to allow the mayor and his staff to pack and distribute them to the local people. I explained that we were helping because there was a significant need, but that the people's need went much deeper than the pit of their stomach. I told him, once again, that true peace only comes from a personal relationship with Jesus Christ. I told him that I wanted to put a copy of the booklet that I wrote about overcoming bitterness and accepting salvation in the hands of all the adults, as well as an illustrated Bible storybook, Good and Evil, in all the houses! He responded, "I will have my staff pack the Good and Evil book, booklets, and tracts in the bags along with the food. That way, every family will be sure to receive them."

I was told that it could not be done. I was told that now is not the time for mass planting of the good seed of the Gospel. I actually believed it. I was left with an impossible dream. Yet God made that impossible dream come true!

Current status: Through the generosity of many people we have currently obtained and moved to the border area 2100 pounds of canned corn, 2500 pounds of canned vegetables, 400 pounds of dried beans, 3500 pounds of rice, as well as lots of bathroom tissue. All of the costs and transportation of these items were either donated or paid for through specific gifts and offerings. There are no outstanding costs involved in getting these items into the hands of the people. They are now stored at the border and will be taken into Mexico on Tuesday.

In addition to these food items, we have seven wheelchairs, eight walkers, and five canes. Some have been shipped to the border and are waiting for pickup along with the food. Others have been acquired in Mexico and will be taken to Ciudad Mier on Monday.

One hundred percent of the cost of acquiring and shipping these items is covered!

The cost of the booklets and tracts on overcoming bitterness and salvation has already been paid as well.

Today we are researching the most economical place to purchase 1100 pounds of cornflower, 1100 pounds of wheat flower, 880 pounds of pasta, 1000 cans of tuna, and 250 liters of vegetable oil. While I do not have the totals yet, it looks like the overall cost of purchasing and shipping will be around $2,300.00. We currently have $780.00 that was given to help cover the cost these items.

I placed an order for 520 copies of the book Good and Evil. Its retail price is $14.95. God placed it on the hearts of the folks at No Greater Joy to help with this project in a significant way. They have made these books available to us for $2.00 each, plus shipping. The total cost of the books will be $1,444.25.

Within the next week all the wheelchairs, walkers, canes, nearly 15,000 pounds of food items, Good and Evil books, tracts, and booklets will be in the hands of people who need them. Seeds are being planted because Believers in Mexico, the United States, and Argentina have come alongside us to help with this impossible dream. Yet, without a doubt, it is God Himself who has orchestrated the events in such a way that this impossible dream is coming true!

I have no idea what God has in store for Ciudad Mier, Presidente Alberto Gonzalez Peña, the military, and us after this big push. Nevertheless, I am waiting with anticipation for the next chapter to be written—perhaps on the tablets of the hearts and lives of many.

After I delivered the food from our church and others in Mexico, I went to Texas to bring in the remaining items that were coming from the USA. At the border crossing, which is less than 20 miles from Ciudad Mier, I had major issues with the woman in charge of importations. Finally, I returned the food to Texas. A few weeks later, I penned the following "private letter." It was an expression of my frustration at "the system" here, but it was never sent. I decided to include it here to demonstrate how difficult the challenges are and how tempting it can be to go with the flow. You must not do that! Stand up and open the path for others to follow.

> I spent the last three days at the border trying to get much-needed food and medical supplies to the people of Mier. During this time, Presidente

Alberto Gonzalez Peña and his staff worked tire-
lessly to help the people whom they serve. The
Presidente has done well in selecting an efficient
and responsive staff. I believe that this administration has been and will continue to be successful in
the eyes of the people as well as in the eyes of
God. The goals of this administration became
clear to me during a conversation that I had with
the director of DIF. She said that, since Don Alberto had taken office, he has been "teaching us
how to serve."

Ciudad Mier is a small town, which has had
more than its share of problems. Last year it was
flooded during hurricane Alex, and then a few
months later a major outbreak of violence began a
major exodus from the city.

In the months following the hurricane and during
the initial attacks, there was help available from the
state of Tamaulipas and from the federal government for the people in need. As always, the help
slowed and then stopped. Don Alberto and his team
were left to fight the battle alone. However, the
state of Tamaulipas has not sent a *single care* package to this area since January, and Mexico City has
not sent a single care package to them this year.

My prayer is that these men, whom God has
placed in authority, come to realize that these issues, along with the violence, must come to the
forefront of their minds and their policies.

There are many inefficiencies and inconsisten-
cies within the border agencies and the local police forces. Please do not get me wrong, I have met
many good and honest people in these areas who
are sincerely trying to help the people within the
guidelines of the law. Nevertheless, others use
and abuse their positions by trying to get dishonest gain for themselves or the government through
misapplication and misinterpretation of the laws.
These people need to be weeded out of the system; they need to be jailed along with the other
criminals!

I know, better than many, that in addition to the local problems, there is a war within the borders of this country. That is one of the reasons that Mier is facing these issues. Thousands of soldiers are stationed near the border. Thousands of men and women are dying every year—many more than are reported. A very small percentage of the situations are actually reported by the media. Armed men stop innocent people regularly. All these issues must not—cannot be addressed separately. They are all part of the same problem and must be addressed simultaneously.

President Felipe Calderón and Governor Egidio Torre Cantú, are you up to the challenge of addressing these issues, along with the violence issues, head on? Let me go a step further. Are you man enough to address these issues openly and publicly with someone like me who has been there and has dealt with the local issues?

Yet the politicians, whether local, state, or national, are not the only ones who need to address these issues. We, as Believers, must also face these issues head on and determine what God would have us to do to help. However, before we can effectively do that, it is imperative that we examine our own lives. For how can we get a speck out of someone else's eye when we have a plank in our own?

Over the last few days, I have been pondering a number of issues that many Believers face throughout the world. Some live in areas where corruption is rampant, scores are confronted with governmental ineptness, and others face rampant misapplication of the law.

What should a Christian do when faced with corruption? How should a Believer respond when confronted by an inept official? What is the appropriate response when a governmental agent is clearly misapplying the law? Believers have struggled throughout the years with these questions. It is not my desire or intent to judge others who may have come to a different conclusion than I have—given their circumstances. It is simply my hope and desire to share what God and others have taught me over the last two decades.

God Uses People Who are Concerned about Lost Souls

There was a lost soul that needed to be saved before the Israelites entered the Promised Land. Her name was Rahab.

> Now Joshua the son of Nun sent out two men from Acacia Grove to spy secretly, saying, "Go, view the land, especially Jericho." So they went, and came to the house of a harlot named Rahab, and lodged there.

—Joshua 2:1

God was not going to judge Jericho until Rahab had been reached. She was told what to do to avoid the judgment that was coming when the Israelites attacked the city. God's heart is always reaching out to save souls. Each soul is precious to Him. God is always concerned for individuals and we should be concerned for them, too.

God uses people who are interested in individuals, not just the masses.

Chapter 7

Turning a Dream into a Reality

A few weeks after a conversation with Daniel and his prayer for us, asking God to provide the money needed to purchase land for the Family Camp, I wrote this letter:

> Years ago on a secular radio program, they were reviewing some unusual statistics. One of them has stuck in my mind throughout all these years: The divorce rate among families who camp together was nearly zero. That is right; the family who camps together stays together!
>
> I have frequently thought of that little tidbit of information: Families who camp together do not divorce.
>
> After mulling it over and over in my mind, I believe that I have determined the underlying effect that causes these families to stay together: Going

camping normally means that the dad is involved! Simply put, the dad who camps is the dad who spends time with his wife and kids. The dad who spends time with his wife and kids is the dad who stays with his wife and kids.

Over sixteen years ago, when we first drove into the valley where I now live in northern Mexico, I thought, "This would be a wonderful place to build a family camp." Now, when I say "Family Camp," I am not talking about your typical retreat center. Let me explain.

Many Mexicans work in factories. While some earn as much as $150 a week, many earn only $60-100 per week. This is a "living wage" in Mexico, but it does not leave much left over for extras. Many factories will give their workers several weeks of paid vacation. However, since they are barely getting by, they do not have funds for vacations or family getaways.

I have prayed about, talked about, and thought about building a family camp—one that would be available free of charge—a place for dads to bring their families for camping and hiking—a place to build memories and relationships. Tent camping to start with, then adding a uniquely designed "fort," teepee camping, and even igloo camping in the highest part of the mountains, plus a few traditional cabins in the lowlands.

A couple of years ago the twelve acres in front of our house came up for sale. As Pam and I were praying, the Lord reminded us of Matthew 13:45-46: "Again, the kingdom of Heaven is like a merchant seeking beautiful pearls; who, when he had found one pearl of great price, went and sold all that he had, and bought it."

Pam and I postponed building our home and purchased the land.

The Lord has now allowed us to finish our home.

Rarely does a week go by that we do not host families here in our home and in the camp. We have had many wonderful family camps this past year as well as several one-day events. Our next event will be an all-night meeting for New Year's Eve. Family camps, marriage retreats, and other special events are becoming the norm, but the focus will always be the same—building families and their relationship with Jesus.

One hundred and ten acres behind our house and an additional one hundred twenty-five acres beside the house are also for sale. The owner of both properties has agreed to sell them for a fair price.

Within two hours of Daniel's prayer, I received an email from a young couple. They had just sent $18,000 designated for land. The following day I received three more emails with funds designated for land!

Several people gave sacrificially and we have all the resources needed for the seventy hectares behind our house! With the remainder of the funds, Pam and I are evaluating two possibilities: begin the needed improvements on the current properties, or put the money toward the last tract of land that flows from the mountain peak on the north side of the valley all the way to the mountain peak on the south side of the valley. This land has a contiguous boundary with about half of the other property.

After considerable thought, we have placed our Ford Excursion for sale in an effort to raise a portion of the needed funds for the purchase of the last tract of land. In addition, we are determined to make the sacrifices that are necessary to purchase the last of the property that the Lord placed in my heart so many years ago. Humanly speaking, that seems like an impossible dream, but perhaps the Lord will allow this impossible dream to become a reality!

A mere two months ago, I thought this deal was dead. Since that time, however, I have seen God's handiwork in amazing ways. Jorge, my neighbor, met with the owner for us and obtained an additional

12% discount on the first property; in addition, the exchange rate took a jump in December, thereby providing some additional funds.

You may have heard me talk about The Caleb Principle—no reserve, no retreat, no regrets. If we give ourselves wholeheartedly to God, He can do the impossible in us and through us. Caleb lived that kind of life. He held nothing back and gave his all to God.

Caleb followed God through many challenges, yet God was always greater than the enemy was! God was greater than the opposition! Caleb chose the land of giants as his reward, and he fought the giants in God's strength! He pursued God's promise!

In Leviticus 19:34 God told the Israelites, "The stranger who dwells among you shall be to you as one born among you, and you shall love him as yourself; for you were strangers in the land of Egypt: I am the LORD your God." In God's providence, this has been our destiny—the Mexican people have adopted us as one of their own. They have become my people!

Caleb rose to the challenge! No enemy was too great, no obstacle was too large, and no opposition too loud to keep Caleb from doing what God wanted him to do. Just as in Caleb, the Spirit of the Living God is raising in me the faith and the courage to stand and fight for the remaining portion of land.

Caleb stood for his faith. Caleb believed that God could and would do the impossible! God was his provision and his power. Caleb spoke of action. Caleb spoke with faith. Caleb lived a different life.

Caleb retained his strength and ability while all others, except Joshua, died in the wilderness. Caleb was rewarded with a new land. Caleb had a different spirit from the rest. He stood tall knowing that he was a son of the King of kings and the Lord of lords!

Caleb's strength was in the Word of God. Caleb's battle-axe was the Word of God! Caleb had a mountain to conquer, and his strength and confidence came from the fact that God had given him His word and promised it to him!

Earlier I wrote, "At forty-seven years of age I walked with a cane due to Multiple Sclerosis. At fifty-two, I was crippled with Spondylitis and required surgery on my neck. During that time, I stood in my wheelchair and preached sitting down with my body racked with pain." I knew beyond a doubt that God had called me to continue preaching the saving message of the Gospel of Jesus Christ.

Today, I stand stronger than I was at forty-seven. I stand today, stronger than I was at fifty-three. I stand on the promises that God has placed deep inside of me. Yes, I have vacillated and wavered, but I know what God has promised to me.

> And now, behold, the LORD has kept me alive, as He said, these forty-five years, ever since the LORD spoke this word to Moses while Israel wandered in the wilderness; and now, here I am this day, eighty-five years old. As yet I am as strong this day as on the day that Moses sent me; just as my strength was then, so now is my strength for war, both for going out and for coming in. Now therefore, give me this mountain of which the LORD spoke in that day.
>
> —Joshua 14:10-12

When I shared this vision with my family, one of my children slipped into my bedroom and placed a little pile of money on my bed along with a note that said, "For the mountain!"

Nearly a year later my little girl was reading the above passage in her private devotion. Not long after that, another little pile of money appeared on my bed with a note that said, "Now therefore, give me this mountain of which the LORD spoke in that day."

> I stand here today facing that mountain that I desire to use to proclaim the Gospel, but I am not alone. My wife, Pam, told me to make the sacrifices needed to purchase the land. My son made significant sacrifices. My daughter did, too. An elder in my local church told me, "Mike, you must buy that mountain." Jorge, a trusted friend in the valley, told me to do the same. Some of you have done the same through sacrificial giving. Another friend here in Mexico wrote, "I believe the Lord has been making changes in your ministry to make it more effective and broader. The possibilities of buying these areas appear to be part of God's plan."

It is no longer just me—a voice crying in the wilderness. *We* stand here and boldly proclaim to the Lord, just as Caleb did, "Now therefore, give me this mountain of which the LORD spoke in that day."

Jorge and I had our final meeting with the owner on January 25, 2015 for finalizing the contract. Everything within me screams that now is the time to move forward.

Thank you for your support and prayers.

We have now purchased both properties debt free and are only waiting for Public Records to issue the final deeds on the properties.

I am convinced that God will do much more than I can ask, or even think, with this land. Following is a story about some of the things that God has already done in and through the family camp.

Baratillo Family Camp

Vivian Bello is the mother of two young daughters. Her family lives in Mexico City. They made the nine-hour trip north to attend our first family camp in 2014.

When we found out that there was going to be a camp at Baratillo, we were excited, not only because we like to go camping, but because we love to learn more about things that relate to our family.

Although initially we thought we would not be able to go, we saw how God began to move the complicated circumstances and He showed us in different ways that we should go. He provided all that was necessary so we would not have to miss out.

Therefore, my husband and I decided to go. In addition to my daughters (a 3-year-old and a 2-month-old), we invited my in-laws, my mother, and, of course, another member of the family who could not be left out—our dog, Zaritza, had to come with us. We prepared by purchasing what was necessary—everything from food to a portable toilet and shower. We also included blankets, a portable gas lamp, clothes, and everything needed for my 2-month-old baby—all the things we needed to have an unbelievable camp experience!

We packed everything into our car. We needed to take so many things that we thought not all of it would fit into the car. We needed space for our dog too; he had to go! After loading and unloading two or three times, everything finally fit. We were really loaded! There was not even a little spot of free space. We had things under the seats, at our feet, and in our laps. This is how our journey started from Mexico City to Saltillo—a long journey for eight people and a dog. The car was filled to our necks, but we knew that God was leading us there!

The trip was very nice but long—9 hours. My 3-year-old daughter, Mer, would ask every five minutes, "Are we almost there?" Although we were all cramped, we were very excited when we finally arrived, full of great expectations.

Once there, everything was fun! We all worked together as a family to prepare the place where we were to stay: beds, food, coolers, blankets, and everything. We still do not know how it all fit into our vehicle.

> *Note by Mike: When I saw how many people, plus a dog, as well as how many things were loaded in their vehicle, I was shocked. I could not believe that they had made the trip riding like that.*

One of the activities was horseback riding, so as soon as we were settled, everybody was off to ride horses! We had a lot of fun, with each waiting for their turn to ride. My mother just had to ride a horse and, of course, my husband, who went galloping away!

> *Note by Mike: Vivian's mom told me, as I was helping her mount the horse, she had ridden as a child and that she was so happy to ride again.*

The meetings were very profitable; I really enjoyed the messages about finances. I now understand that it is very important to teach our children to work from an early age and to hold them accountable for the money they make. I also learned that even young kids can learn to do hard things with God's direction and His wisdom. Each message was edifying to me. My husband said that those were the most complete and deep teachings that he had ever heard! He continues to listen to the recordings so they continue to be a blessing to my family.

> *Note by Anna Richardson (17): Our church, La Iglesia de Baratillo, had the first family camp during*

Easter week. I helped with the registration of the families, making sure they knew the ground rules and where to set up camp. Because of this, I was able to personally meet and spend time with each family. I had met the Bello family on other occasions, but never had spent much one-on-one time with them until the family camp. Throughout the week, I helped Vivian with Annette, their new baby, changing diapers and holding her during the meeting so Vivian could listen to the messages. I also enjoyed playing with and watching Merari, their 3-year-old daughter. Mer told me that she wanted to learn to speak English. So I spent time teaching her some simple phrases and words in English, and found that she already had quite a large vocabulary. She really just needed help with how to put the words she knew into practice.

Jonathan asked Daddy if I could go home with them at the end of the week, for about a month to continue working with Mer. He said no at that time but about a month later, after a conference in Pachuca, I was able to spend about four weeks with their family in Mexico City. It was my first time being away from home without any family, so it was quite a new experience! During the mornings, my teaching mostly included playing with the girls, teaching them actions by actually performing them. "Run" was not just a word; it was an action.

I did my own school in the evening. I enjoyed not only getting to know this family better, but also was able to better appreciate the work that goes into teaching a child. I grew to love the Bello Family like my own family, and really appreciate the time they invested in my life, and the way they opened their heart and home to me, treating me like one of their own.

During the campfire, there were some special moments, not only because of the delicious marshmallows, but because there was harmonious warmth, where together we shared special moments.

My father and sister came from Monterrey on Saturday afternoon, planning to be there just for a short time. Because they felt so well received by the hospitality of the Richardsons, they ended up spending the night with us.

I was very happy because all my family was together: my parents, my sister, my husband and his parents and, of course, my daughters. It is a great blessing to partake of an event like this, where we are exhorted to allow Christ to shine in our families; God has started to do that in us. Since my parents were divorced when I was a child, this was the first time in many years that we were all together.

On Sunday we went to the church meeting. We were all blessed and, at the end of the meeting, my dad said, "I want to follow Jesus." That was a miracle since only in very few occasions had he been to a Christian church but, after speaking with Brother Mike, he began to understand many things. I know God is continuing what He started in my dad. My mother was touched by the good testimony of the Richardson family; her heart was touched. She learned about forgiveness and love. Today, my mother's salvation is a reality.

We all returned home very blessed, assured that when we allow God's hand to lead us, the blessings will not be long in arriving.
   —Vivian Bello

Six months after the family camp, Vivian's mother was taken to a hospital in Monterrey. She was very sick. Pam visited her once and then we both visited a second time. I have asked Pam to write this part of the story.

Note by Pam: When I went to visit Doña Juanita in the hospital, I was shocked at her physical condition. She was very weak and could not sit up. She spoke in a whisper.

The last time we had talked was in my home during the family camp. She had poured out her heart; she had a very difficult life. We talked about forgiveness and restoration. I asked her if she was willing to forgive her estranged husband, who had abandoned her more than 20 years ago. I also asked if she was willing for the Lord to restore her marriage if that was His will. Neither of them had remarried. She told me that was impossible and that it would never work.

When her ex-husband showed up unexpectedly later in the day, she was very shocked and furious that he was there. When she told me about all the pain she had been through with him, she was not expecting to see him later that day in my home. As he sat at the counter with one of their daughters and me, she lashed out at him in anger. He just got up and walked outside. Then her daughter also got up and walked away.

I told her that if she let this anger control her, she would damage her relationship with her children. She began to cry bitterly and told me it already had damaged their relationship.

The next morning, she cried through the whole service, came, and told me that God had brought her to the family camp just for this. She was making things right with the Lord, while God was working in the heart of her ex-husband at the same time.

As I approached her hospital bed, she immediately began to tell me she had forgiven her husband and God was restoring her relationship with him. She said she loved him and he told her that he loved her. He stayed several nights at the hospital to help care for her. He told his children he loved her like the Bible said in 1 Corinthians 13.

Juanita's body did not leave the hospital, but her spirit is now with the Lord. She spent her last days reconciling relationships and left a legacy for her children and a great example for me.

This is what the family camp is all about—impacting the lives of people.

Chapter 8

Establishing a Financial Plan

For the Believer, planning is an indispensable component in the development of a financial strategy. This is really the process of learning to be responsible for yourself, your family, and your finances.

> Through wisdom a house is built, and by understanding it is established; by knowledge the rooms are filled with all precious and pleasant riches.

> —Proverbs 24:3-4

You must learn to plan your way—the dreams for your future—but your plans must allow enough flexibility to follow the direction of the Lord. Many times, He will direct your paths in ways that you had not planned. Following His direction will require a changed attitude on your part. That changed attitude is flexibility.

Many people "put their hands to the plow," develop a financial plan, and then hide it away in a drawer. You must use your plans to guide your decisions every day.

Make Wise Plans

Patience, orderliness, and excellence are key factors in every area of life—especially finances! Make wise plans and avoid making hasty changes to those plans, but do not close your ears to the still, small voice of the Spirit of God. For, you see, many times that quiet voice will lead you to greater heights than you have ever imagined!

> My brethren, count it all joy when you fall into
> various trials, knowing that the testing of your
> faith produces patience.
>
> —James 1:2-3

The Plan

There are two types of plans that must be considered: long-range and short-range plans.

Establish a written plan. It will not only help you achieve your goals but will also motivate you to work more diligently to obtain them. This written plan is a budget. Some people believe that a budget confines them and limits their freedom, but that is not the case. As you learn and apply practical ideas related to handling the resources placed in your hands by God, He will give you wisdom. It is when those practical concepts are combined with godly wisdom that you will begin to realize that, along with His wisdom, He has given you a peace that passes all understanding. No more worrying about annual taxes, clothes, and other bills that come once or twice a year. Your budget prepares you for them. Over time, you will find that a budget gives you more freedom—not less.

Commit Your Works to the Lord

The first step is to commit your works to the Lord. If you will do that then He will help you to establish your thoughts and goals. It is your God-given responsibility to plan and if you do so with a right attitude, then God promises that He will direct your steps.

Attention to Detail

Patience, endurance, and stamina, mixed with attention to detail, will certainly make the difference in your success or failure in the area of finances.

> A man's heart plans his way, But the LORD directs his steps.
>
> —Proverbs 16:9

A few years ago, my wife received a note that clearly demonstrates the importance of listening to that still, small voice of the Lord. I will share it with you.

God Has Hands

Did you know that God has hands? Well, He does. They are borrowed. Nevertheless, He uses them to bless and heal and meet needs. Want to see them? Look at the end of your arms.

Friday afternoon, we had a couple of handfuls of flour, some summer squash, two cans of green beans, and odds & ends of seasonings in the house. The Garza family was to come and spend Friday night and Saturday with us. I had told God earlier that it was up to Him, and I would wait to see His deliverance, so I did. He sent three big boxes of deliverance right on time, using borrowed hands, and blessed me and gave my children a visual aid to their present memory passage (Luke 12:22-31). May I please say thank you with a whole heart?

From now on your title is "God's Little Helper."

Financial Planning is a Key Element

As a young couple looking forward to marriage, you must make financial planning a key element *before* marriage. Get started on a firm foundation. Learn to talk, to communicate effectively in this area before marriage, and it will jump-start effective communication in all areas of life after marriage.

> Counsel in the heart of man is like deep water,
> but a man of understanding will draw it out.
>
> —Proverbs 20:5

It is the responsibility of both of you to "draw out" the deep inner thoughts, feeling, concerns, and worries of the other, so that they can be discussed in an open and honest manner.

There are some short-range plans that must be completed before marriage. First, you must either have a house or have enough money to set up a household. I am not saying that you must own a home; it is fine to rent a home. When you marry, a man must leave his father and mother. It will almost always be a disaster if he simply brings his wife to his parents' home to live. You must be prepared to set up a home BEFORE marriage. In addition, the husband must be earning enough money to support a wife and child. Children are a blessing from the Lord; therefore, it is reasonable to expect that it is possible that the Lord will send a child into your home within the first year of marriage. He may not, but you must be prepared should He choose to bless your home in that way.

These same concepts apply to a married couple. Draw out the depths of your spouse's heart as you begin the process of short-range planning.

Short-range plans will include things like buying clothes, food, transportation, electricity, vacations, gifts, and any other expense that occurs during a twelve-month period.

It is important to note that, if your budget provokes irritation and conflict, then you did not do the planning well. One spouse, most often the husband, is trying to force his will on the wife. Start over, listen to each other, and work out the differences. Once you develop a budget that works for both husband and wife, you will find that all the work was well worth the effort.

Traditions

For the young couple or the family with limited income, you may need to eliminate traditions that many families have—like gift giving at Christmas time. This year, something interesting happened in my home. Pam came to me and told me about a conversation that our children had and the decision that they themselves made. Before I tell you that story, let me give you some background. We have ten children. Five of them still live at home. The ones at home range from eighteen down to seven years old. Earlier in the year, I had suggested that we stop buying certain food items because our income was down. I did not cut out my wife's favorite foods. All of these items were things that I really liked— including bacon. Now when you read that, you might come to the false conclusion that I am becoming a health nut—wrong! I love bacon, but the cost per pound is very high so I made a financial decision to stop buying it.

Now our family tradition at Christmas time has been to have a Christmas bag for each child that contained some candy and a few small presents—perhaps a deck of cards, a flashlight or a pocketknife. In addition to that, we would buy the kids some practical gifts, like pants or shirts, that they would need even if it were not Christmas, plus something that was special for them. Some years it might be larger than other years. Since we live in a remote area in northern Mexico, one year, Joshua received a calf. Other times it might be a toy or a special pair of earrings.

Now, let me get back to the story. Our five children living at home, ages eighteen to seven, got together and decided to ask us not to buy them any presents this year for Christmas! They recognized our financial situation and all agreed that this would be the best option for our family. A seven-year-old understood that concept without Momma or Daddy talking to them. A seven-year-old and four of her siblings all understood it! I do not even know which child, or children, first came up with the idea. They spoke with one voice.

If a seven-year-old can understand the concept of spending less than you make and take steps to apply it in her life, why can you not do the same?

Short-Range Plans

There are a number of steps to establishing short-range plans. While some of these steps might be different depending on your family's unique circumstances, I believe that Larry Burkett identified most, if not all, of those that are essential for all Christian families.

He lists the steps to short-range planning as:

- Establish written plans and goals.
- Commit God's portion first.
- Reduce or eliminate the use of debt.
- Seek God's plan [direction] for living within the budget.
- Set your own goals.
- Seek good Christian counsel.

Larry's teaching has affected my life in more ways than I can explain. In this section about planning, I will simply talk with you about the things that I learned so many years ago when I first went through his study titled, "How to Manage Your Money." When we moved to Mexico in 1993, we left most of our possessions behind. But Larry's teaching had impacted my life in such a profound way that it came with me—in my heart and in writing as well. I will lean heavily on his teachings in this section. In his unique teaching style, he would present the truths in God's Word and help his students to draw their own conclusions from those verses. It is for that reason that I will use the same verses that he used when teaching me about setting goals more than three decades ago. I will also share with you my conclusions from those verses, but it is my hope, my prayer, that you will not just read my conclusions and accept them as the final say on these verses. Read them. Meditate on them. Ask God to open your eyes and your heart to the deepness and the fullness of His Word for your life. Ask His Spirit to reveal the meaning and the application for your life—for God's calling in your life. Establish written plans and goals.

> **Commit your works to the LORD, and your thoughts will be established.**

> **—Proverbs 16:3**

Seeking God with a whole heart should be the first step in every area of life. If you want His blessing, seek Him and you will find Him. Seek His will and He will not hide it from you. This applies to every area of life, including, but not limited to, finances. Seek Him individually; seek Him as a couple. Then He will bring unity and balance into your plans. You may find that He gives you part of the plan for your life and part to your spouse. You are both necessary elements in effectively planning your life's goals and the use of the resources that God entrusts to your family.

A man's heart plans his way, but the LORD directs his steps.

—Proverbs 16:9

It is your responsibility to study, to pray, and to seek God. It is also your responsibility to plan for the path that you believe God is showing you. Then as you walk down that path, as you follow through on each step, you must trust that God will lead, direct, and guide every step. Oh, that is the hard part—trusting God every moment of every day of your life. Your inner man will cry out to be in control. Fallen nature is that way—it wants to control. Nevertheless, you must gain victory in this area. Let God be in control. Cede that right to God. Learn to depend upon His Word. In order to do so you must grow in faith, and in order to grow in faith you must never forget the powerful and life-changing words found in Romans 10:17.

So then faith comes by hearing, and hearing by the word of God.

—Romans 10:17

If you can understand the deepness and the fullness of God's Word, then, and only then, will you begin to grasp the role that He plays in your plans and in your life! "A man's heart plans his way, but the LORD directs his steps" (Proverbs 16:9).

Keep Written Journals

Begin by keeping two written journals of what you spend. One will be kept by the wife and the other will be kept by the husband. Record everything in the journals for a month. This will give you a basis from which you can begin forming your budget. Now it is important to note that some expenses will not be listed. If the car did not break down, then there will not be any car repair listed. These types of expenses are variable expenses. You must calculate the annual cost of each variable expense and allow for it in your monthly budget.

Your financial plan is designed to tell you when you have spent what you planned to spend. When you reach the end of your planned spending, you must either stop spending in that area or make a conscious decision about where the money will come from—which area you are going to sacrifice to continue spending in the other area. If you do not do so, it will certainly lead to debt.

Commit God's Portion First

Later I will talk more in-depth on both tithes and offerings, but it is important to lay down a few foundational points here in this section on planning. For, you see, if you want God to honor your plans, you must honor Him. He tells us this in His Word!

> Honor the LORD with your possessions, and with the first fruits of all your increase; so your barns will be filled with plenty, and your vats will over-flow with new wine.

> —Proverbs 3:9-10

For many, perhaps most, this is a hard concept to apply. For some reason that I cannot explain, our financial resources and our control of them somehow make us think that we are something more than we really are. Honoring God and obeying the Biblical concept of tithing helps us to overcome the pride that comes with the love of money.

How you handle your finances is simply an outside indicator of what is on the inside—in your heart. If you do not honor God with your first fruits, repent and begin to do so, and you will find that God will begin to pour out spiritual blessings upon you and your family.

> If we have sown spiritual things for you, is it a great thing if we reap your material things?

> —2 Corinthians 9:11

If you rent a house, you pay the rent. If you buy groceries, you pay for them. If you take a taxi, you pay the driver. Is it really such a big thing to bless those who minister to you with material things?

Reduce or Eliminate the Use of Debt

A prudent man foresees evil and hides himself;
the simple pass on and are punished.

—Proverbs 27:12

The concepts of this verse when related to debt and bondage are clear. The better option for any couple is to avoid the use of debt from the very beginning of your life together!

Seek God's Plan [Direction] for Living Within the Budget

Learn discipline and live within your income. It is that simple! Stop using credit to buy gasoline or gifts or groceries.

When you first begin to make your financial plans, it is likely that you will find that the paycheck ends before the month ends. There are two solutions—earn more or spend less. I propose that you must first learn to live within the income that you have now before you look for other ways to earn more money.

Why?

Well first, the Bible teaches us to be content in whatever state we are in at that moment. Secondly, the temptation is to send the wife out to work in order to bring in more income, and this is the road to disaster in the lives of many families. More money coming in usually just leads to more money going out.

Once you learn to live within your means, then it is easier for you to evaluate the current situation and decide if God is really leading you to look for a different job or an additional job or not.

In our life, Pam and I have seen the Lord provide for our needs through means other than purchasing them. If we had borrowed when the need first arose, we would have eliminated the opportunity to see God work in our lives in real and practical ways. Other times we have saved, over time, for purchases. Either way God's hand is at work in our lives. We must learn to trust Him!

Rest in the LORD, and wait patiently for Him; do not
fret because of him who prospers in his way, because
of the man who brings wicked schemes to pass.

—Psalm 37:7

It is God's desire to bless those who seek Him. Seek Him, lean on Him! Pray about every area of your finances and about each purchase. Nothing is too little or too big to pray about—not even diapers!

> For the eyes of the LORD run to and fro throughout the whole earth, to show Himself strong on behalf of those whose heart is loyal to Him. In this you have done foolishly; therefore, from now on you shall have wars.

> —2 Chronicles 16:9

Set Your Own Goals

Do not just accept others' goals as your own. Proverbs 14:15 tells us, "The simple believes every word, But the prudent considers well his steps." God can and will direct you. Yes, He uses counselors, but they do not make the decisions for you. They give advice and then leave the result to God and you. It is important to note that you can get a lot of dumb financial counsel from fine Christians. Listen to counsel, and then make wise and informed decisions.

God has a plan for your life. Do not allow yourself to be caught up in things just because others are doing it. Many times men get caught up in the "status symbol" created by the type of car they drive. Be very careful not to fall in this type of trap! Set your own goals and make your primary goal to become more like Jesus every day of your life.

> As for me, I will see Your face in righteousness; I shall be satisfied when I awake in Your likeness.

> —Psalm 17:15

Be content with what you have and seek the wisdom that is from God. "Godliness with contentment is great gain!" (1 Timothy 6:6).

> Happy is the man who finds wisdom, and the man who gains understanding; for her proceeds are

better than the profits of silver, and her gain than
fine gold.

—Proverbs 3:13-14

God founded the earth by wisdom; therefore, wisdom is a good
foundation. Use it as a foundation for your life, your marriage, your
finances, and your relationship with the Lord. Seek Him and His
will and you will find both.

The LORD by wisdom founded the earth; by understanding, He established the heavens.

—Proverbs 3:19

Seek Good Christian Counsel

Listen to counsel and receive instruction, that you
may be wise in your latter days.

—Proverbs 19:20

We are wise when we seek counsel. We are wiser when we seek
counsel from a variety of counselors. It is important that the
counselors be good counselors. For, you see, if you seek the counsel
of a fool, you will make foolish decisions!

Blessed is the man who walks not in the counsel
of the ungodly, nor stands in the path of sinners,
nor sits in the seat of the scornful.

—Psalm 1:1

I think that it is prudent to note that, after you receive counsel,
you are the one responsible for evaluating it and making the
decision!

Since we should seek wise counsel and since wisdom comes from
God, we should look at Scripture to see whose counsel we should
seek—father, mother, spouse, pastor, elders, and other Believers
who meet the qualifications of an elder would be wise counselors
as well.

Listen to your father who begot you, and do not despise your mother when she is old.

—Proverbs 23:22

For the husband is head of the wife, as also Christ is head of the church; and He is the Savior of the body.

—Ephesians 5:23

For this reason a man shall leave his father and mother and be joined to his wife, and the two shall become one flesh.

—Ephesians 5:31

Where there is no counsel, the people fall; but in the multitude of counselors there is safety.

—Proverbs 11:14

If a man is blameless, the husband of one wife, having faithful children not accused of dissipation or insubordination. For a bishop must be blameless, as a steward of God, not self-willed, not quick-tempered, not given to wine, not violent, not greedy for money, but hospitable, a lover of what is good, sober-minded, just, holy, self-controlled, holding fast the faithful word as he has been taught, that he may be able, by sound doctrine, both to exhort and convict those who contradict.

—Titus 1:6-9

Shepherd the flock of God which is among you, serving as overseers, not by compulsion but willingly, not for dishonest gain but eagerly; nor as being lords over those entrusted to you, but being examples to the flock.

—1 Peter 5:2-3

Characteristics of Those Who Plan Their Way

Knowledge, self-control, perseverance, godliness, brotherly kindness, and love will be the characteristics of those who learn to plan their way and then yield their right to direct each step to God.

Downfalls

One of the biggest financial downfalls for young couples today is the desire to get too much too soon. The bankers and lenders of this generation no longer try to keep people in check financially as they did in years gone by. Credit card companies and other lenders charge high interest rates, expecting that some will not repay; yet knowing that because of the rates that they are charging they will still make a significant profit. The ease with which families can take out loans has led many down the road of despair and destruction.

Long-Range Plans

While we are on the topic of planning and budgeting, I think that it would be appropriate to turn our thoughts to long-range planning.

When I am preaching, I probably quote Hebrew 12:1-2 more than any other verse (except Romans 10:17).

> Therefore we also, since we are surrounded by so great a cloud of witnesses, let us lay aside every weight, and the sin which so easily ensnares us, and let us run with endurance the race that is set before us, looking unto Jesus, the author and finisher of our faith, who for the joy that was set before Him endured the cross, despising the shame, and has sat down at the right hand of the throne of God.
>
> —Hebrews 12:1-2

Our ultimate long-range plan needs to be looking forward with great anticipation to the day that we finish the race we have here on this earth, and to take as many people as possible with us. That, however, is the topic of another book. Now, I would like to turn our attention to long-range financial planning.

Your long-term plans are simply a series of short-term plans placed end to end. Where do you want to be in ten or twenty years? If you do not make those goals and then plan a path to achieve them, ultimately you will get what you planned for—a wasted life!

Planning is necessary, but even the best of plans will fail without follow-up.

Too many couples begin by setting minimum goals. Then when God blesses them financially, the goals grow with the income and there never seems to be any left over. I believe that God would prefer to see his people establishing maximum goals. What size home do you need, how much money do you need in the bank for the unexpected, how much is needed in reserves for your latter years? If you will set these goals in these areas ahead of time, then you will know without a doubt that any extra that comes into your hands is meant for another purpose. That purpose might be to advance God's kingdom by helping to fund mission work. It might be to help your church with a special project, or to help a family with special needs, or one of the many other needs that are being left unmet in the body of Christ because many churches have become greedy for gain.

God has raised up people all over the world to help meet the needs of the saints. Are you included in that number?

> **Let them do good, that they be rich in good works, ready to give, willing to share, storing up for themselves a good foundation for the time to come, that they may lay hold on eternal life.**
>
> **—1 Timothy 6:18-19**

You must learn to be rich in good works. You must be ready to give.

Standard of Living

Establish the standard of living for your family ahead of time. This could be called a family living plan. God is a rewarder, not a punisher. Your family does not have to suffer.

What is God's plan for your life? Ask in faith—believing! "God, I desire the best. You know what is best. Help me to yield all areas of my life to Your will. Help me to do it cheerfully. Help me to understand."

Establish a family sharing plan, too. Give into the lives of people and you will see the results of your investments.

> He answered and said to them, "He who has two tunics, let him give to him who has none; and he who has food, let him do likewise."

> —Luke 3:11

Sharing what we have with those in need is God's plan. He gives many Believers surplus so that they can meet the needs of others, and, in turn, the name of the Lord will be glorified. God frequently provides what someone needs though another. Invest in the Kingdom of God. Go to the ant and learn from it. When the ant has a surplus, it saves it, but the ant does not hoard! Do not hoard!

> Do not let your adornment be merely outward— arranging the hair, wearing gold, or putting on fine apparel—rather let it be *the hidden person of the heart*, with the incorruptible beauty of a gentle and quiet spirit, which is very precious in the sight of God.

> —1 Peter 3:3-4

When your family knows and understands your long-term goals, then they will understand the boundaries and limits that they need to live within and will help you stop overspending.

Scripture does not rule out having things, but it is important that those things not just be for appearance sake. When I was reviewing this verse with my son Samuel, he said, "That is like our friend from San Antonio. He has a lot of nice things and a nice home but he freely opens them up to many people—sharing them with others."

A father is responsible for his family—even if he dies. If you die without a will, you let the state decide what is best for your family. That is wrong, unless you are familiar with your state's law regarding how estates are distributed, and that distribution law meets your plan.

Death

If the husband died today, can the wife take care of the finances? If not, then the husband has work to do in order to prepare his family in the event that he dies before the wife. If the wife dies first, does the husband know what is needed to manage the family's finances? If not, then again, work is needed.

While the latter is not the case in our home, I added it since in many one-income families, it is the wife who pays the bills and keeps the records since she has more time at home to do so. Let me also mention, while the husband is the one ultimately responsible for making sure that the family's finances are in order, if your wife has a greater gift in this area, you would be wise to ask her to help you with the task of paying the bills and keeping the records. She is, after all, your helpmeet!

College

What about the cost of college for the children? Some families feel that they must do whatever is necessary to provide for the cost of a college education. Other families feel that it is best for the children to work their way through college. Make your decision early. Then plan for it and prepare your children for their part in that decision.

If you do not have goals, you will never reach them. Your plans should be written so that you can review them periodically. Establish your maximum goals. If you simply spend more because you have more, you consider yourself an owner, not a steward. This, however, does not mean you have to live like a pauper.

Just as God is orderly and consistent, you need to strive for that in all areas of your life—including finances. Financial planning is essential for success in handling your finances. These principles are the foundation for successful Christian living. Success will require a changed attitude—today and every day of your life.

Chapter 9

Your Attitude Makes All
the Difference

I have always found the passage in Luke that says "Mary his es-
poused wife, being great with child" to be very interesting. Having had ten children of our own, I realize that, when my wife is
"great with child," something exciting is about to happen—that
which we have longed for is about to take place. Being "great
with child" really indicates a two-step process. There will be a
significant amount of labor to bring forth the blessing. Then
there will be substantial volumes of work to bring that child to
maturity.

In much the same way, developing and implementing a budget
not only requires dedicated labor upfront but also requires
consistent work day-by-day and week-by-week in order to
effectively carry out the plan that you establish for your family.

In our study on finances, it is important that we not only look at
why we should make money, but also how we should use it and
how we should spend it. Money can provide comfort and ease.

Money can make life more convenient. It can also be the means for spreading the Gospel of Jesus Christ. Sadly, money can go far beyond any of these things. For many people, money has become their idol.

The love of money can separate families. I have seen many families torn apart because one sibling did not get the inheritance that they thought they deserved. The love of money can spoil children by getting everything handed to them and never learning the value of a hard day's work. The love of money can breed dishonesty among businessmen, church leaders, and everyday folk alike. No one is exempt.

Inheritance

Consider giving an inheritance to your children while you are living—while you can help direct them in using it, rather than waiting until you die.

Since the love of money can cause great devastation in your life, it is vitally important to know why God would have us, as Christians, accumulate wealth.

The Ministry of Giving

There are many ministry gifts given to the church body. Most Believers have multiple gifts. One of those gifts is a ministry based in money—the ministry of giving!

This is where your attitude comes into play for, you see, God loves a cheerful giver.

> So let each one give as he purposes in his heart, not grudgingly or of necessity; for God loves a cheerful giver.
>
> —2 Corinthians 9:7

If you give grudgingly, you have lost the greatest blessing in giving—a cheerful heart. Get your heart right with God and then give! The verse that follows is very interesting.

> And God is able to make all grace abound toward you, that you, always having all sufficiency in all

things, may have an abundance for every good work.

—2 Corinthians 9:8

Once you recognize the ministry of giving with a cheerful heart and put it into practice in your life, God says that you will not only have sufficient, but an abundance from which you can give!

Paul told Timothy, in 1 Timothy 6:18, "Let them do good, that they be rich in good works, ready to give, willing to share." Now I want you to think about this verse for a moment. How many times did your mother tell you exactly the same thing—be good and share?

Giving Versus Getting

Believers often think of giving as godly, but gaining (earning a profit) as wrong. In order to give, one must first have something from which they can give—the profit that they earned. Accept that principle and ingrain it into your personality. Making a fair profit allows you to be generous and give! A workman is worthy of his hire!

I fear that in the area of Christian conferences, some in Mexico, perhaps many, have wrongly misunderstood my stance about charging for conferences. Many years ago, when I first began the conferences of EL Hogar Educador, Pam and I made the decision not to charge for those conferences. That was a personal conviction for us that we continue today. We do not charge for conferences, nor do I ever charge for preaching.

That is one of our areas of giving. Nevertheless, it is wrong for someone to take our conviction and expect someone else to offer their conferences free of charge. They are providing a valuable service to you. Expect to pay for it! Honor them. Do not gripe and fuss because you have to pay! A workman is worthy of his hire.

These same principles apply to any secular business. Do not expect a discount because the mechanic is a Brother in Christ. Do not expect a discount because the hair stylist is a Believer. Expect to pay a fair price for a good product! Oh, they may give you a discount, but do not ever go to them expecting it. Expect to pay full price every time!

Attitudes and Motives

When I sat down to talk with my son, Samuel, about the attitudes and motives that the world has for accumulating wealth, he listed the following:

- Security
- Comfort
- Nest egg
- Saving for a rainy day
- Importance or status

As we tried to line those up with God's reasons, we found that only the first—security—could loosely be aligned with provision for the family. The rest of the world's reason for accumulating wealth seemed to be completely out of line with God's Word.

Many people make investments and attempt to accumulate money simply because others advise them to do so. It is important to note that Proverbs 14:15 is the balancing verse of Proverbs 15:22.

The simple believes every word, but the prudent considers well his steps.

—Proverbs 14:15

Without counsel, plans go awry, but in the multitude of counselors they are established.

—Proverbs 15:22

We are to seek counsel, but we are not to simply believe every word spoken to us. Evaluate the advice, pray about it, research it, and then dismiss the advice that will lead you astray!

Envy

Many people seek wealth and try to accumulate money because they envy others. While some might call it "social pressure," God calls it "covetousness and greed." Too many times, Believers become envious when they see the prosperity of the wicked. This is nothing but a slippery slope that leads down to the pit.

And He said to them, "Take heed and beware of covetousness, for one's life does not consist in the abundance of the things he possesses."

—Luke 12:15

Envy also limits our usefulness to God. Once we allow envy and covetousness to enter our hearts, we become of little use as a testimony for our Lord.

Winner Takes All

Many people attempt to accumulate money as if it were a game. Everyone becomes a potential client—family, friends, and fellow Believers alike. With the advent of the internet, social media, and multilevel marketing, this money-making game seems to have gotten worse. I say "seems" because the underlying attitude has always been there, but with the ease of communication it is able to surface more easily. It is unfortunate that the church as a whole seems to elevate the "winners"—those making the most money. The game continues at a never-ending rate until it ends in a "no holds barred" contest.

One characteristic found in this type of business is the inability to accept a loss. Another is the unwillingness to help someone who has a true need. The profit becomes king. The "winners" are crowned for their earning—the love of money rules and reigns. If you see these trappings, avoid them no matter how much money you see others earning.

Let a man meet a bear robbed of her cubs, rather than a fool in his folly.

—Proverbs 17:12

Self-Esteem

Many people attempt to accumulate money for their own self-esteem. They purchase the "right" kind of clothes and associate with the "right" kind of people. They only give to be recognized. The only thing that they love more than their money is themselves!

Command those who are rich in this present age
not to be haughty, nor to trust in uncertain riches
but in the living God, who gives us richly all
things to enjoy.

—1 Timothy 6:17

Pride goes before destruction, and a haughty
spirit before a fall.

—Proverbs 16:18

Attitude and Motives

Money is neither good nor bad. It is the use of it—our attitude and our motives toward it—that counts.

Many people attempt to accumulate money because of the love of money and they will not part with it for any reason! They are the hoarders of the world. They may have much, but the loss of even a little will be terribly disturbing to them. Their life is full of greed accompanied by bitterness.

For the love of money is a root of all kinds of evil,
for which some have strayed from the faith in
their greediness, and pierced themselves
through with many sorrows.

—1 Timothy 6:10

The sad thing is that their money will not satisfy their desires, nor will any increase in their riches satisfy them. They are in a never-ending cycle of wanting more and more and more. In the end, perhaps on their deathbed, they will find out that it is all vanity.

Protection

Many people attempt to accumulate money for protection. The obsession with protection in today's society takes away a key element of the Christian life: living by faith. At first, the goal is just a few thousand dollars, but then the mind runs wild with the potential uncertainties. There is never enough protection! Yet God says that He will deliver us in the day of trouble. Again, there is nothing inherently wrong with planning and saving within the guidelines in Scripture, but we must be very wary of hoarding.

God promises His blessings to all who share freely. Accumulate money to give. Give generously.

> But this I say: He who sows sparingly will also
> reap sparingly, and he who sows bountifully will
> also reap bountifully.
>
> —2 Corinthians 9:6

The principle of sowing and reaping is a universal principle. Sow a little; reap a small harvest. Sow abundantly; reap an abundant harvest. As you sow through giving, be sure to water the soil with the right attitudes and correct motives. They will be like the water and rain that will ensure an abundant crop in your life. God loves a cheerful giver.

Chapter 10

Do I Have Enough?

Obedience brings many blessings in our lives. Obedience in the area of finances will bring about a peace that passes all understanding. Each of us is making financial decisions every day about spending or saving and, hopefully, about sharing the resources that God has placed into our hands. Families try to accumulate money for a vast number of reasons. I would like to look at several of these motives and try to help you find the answer to the question, how much is enough? As you read this chapter, it is of utmost importance that you keep Proverbs 15:16 at the forefront of your mind.

> Better is a little with the fear of the LORD, than
> great treasure with trouble.
>
> —Proverbs 15:16

How Much Cash Should I Have on Hand for Current Needs?

This amount will vary greatly from family to family, but we must face the fact that we live in a consumptive society that tends to live from paycheck to paycheck. It does not matter how much money you make, you will never have enough until you decide to live on what you have available. Most people can get by on what they make if they make a commitment to do so. We must decide how much we are going to live on and then do it. It may need to be adjusted from time to time as prices increase and your life's situations change.

Current needs are the sum of your current standard of living plus a reasonable amount of short-term cash reserves. I believe that it is appropriate to set aside about 5% each month. While current needs do differ from family to family, we must all follow the guidelines that God has set down in Scripture. Those who fail to make provision to meet the current needs of their family are clearly outside of God's will. They and their families will suffer as a result.

You must pray about it until you determine what God has for your life. Balance is one of the main principles that you must consider.

> I went by the field of the lazy man, and by the vineyard of the man devoid of understanding; and there it was, all overgrown with thorns; its surface was covered with nettles; its stone wall was broken down. When I saw it, I considered it well; I looked on it and received instruction: A little sleep, a little slumber, a little folding of the hands to rest; So shall your poverty come like a prowler, And your need like an armed man.
>
> —Proverbs 24:30-34

The main characteristic described here is laziness. Laziness gives birth to slothfulness, which results in hunger. Take a moment and examine yourself. Ask yourself, "Am I lazy? Do I try to get out of work, or do I jump in and do it?"

If, in your honest evaluation, you concluded that you really do have lazy tendencies, then stop reading right now and confess it to the Lord and ask Him with a sincere heart to help you overcome this in your life. He will!

> Whoever loves instruction loves knowledge, but he who hates correction is stupid.
>
> —Proverbs 12:1

Prosperity will come as a result of being diligent in your work.

> The rich man's wealth is his strong city, and like a high wall in his own esteem.

—Proverbs 18:11

Riches and wealth are really just an imaginary protection from life's adversities. Sadly, many have found out too late that it can all be gone in a moment. Our faith and confidence must be in the Lord.

> But woe to you who are rich, for you have received your consolation. Woe to you who are full, for you shall hunger. Woe to you who laugh now, for you shall mourn and weep.

—Luke 6:24-25

Many people have said that, while riches do not bring happiness, it sure does make being sad more enjoyable. That is simply not true. If one is not content with what they have, they will never be content with more. Wealth without godliness brings about anguish and despair.

In order to build a lifestyle that brings happiness and fulfillment, you must look into the Word of God. It will give you life more abundantly! Let us take a quick look at six principles that will make a good foundation for any family when developing a life plan.

Six Principles for Success

Slothfulness is not acceptable in the life of the Believer. Slothfulness is an unwillingness to work or apply one's self. A sloth is just plain lazy and does not want to be responsible for anything. Slothfulness goes far beyond laziness; it also means an apathy or failure to care.

The slothful person just wants to have fun. Avoiding responsibilities and household tasks is part of his lifestyle. When things go wrong (because he ignored them), he will often try to make himself look better by placing the blame on others. Others have to take care of his responsibilities, adding an extra load on their shoulders. Many times, they must accept the sloth's responsibilities or the family will perish.

Many wives have gone to work to pay the rent and put food on the table because their husbands were sloths and simply would not provide for the needs of the family.

A little slothfulness evolves into much slothfulness. It is habit forming and touches the lives of many families. When there is much slothfulness, things remain undone or unfinished, and even the house starts to fall apart, decaying for lack of care while the sloth is out having fun or sleeping his life away. His obligations fall on everybody but him.

The sloth will be evasive in order to protect his slothfulness. He does not want anyone to inquire about his activities or even his intentions so his deceits will not be revealed. If someone does manage to get close and begin to reveal the truth, the sloth will react by becoming angry. This is his way of trying to regain control. If that does not work, he will simply shut down and go silent.

Slothfulness is a deadly trap that kills any motivation to repent. In order to gain freedom, he must make strong efforts to be diligent in everything and to do it all as unto the Lord.

Slothfulness is not acceptable in the life of the Believer and must be avoided in order to build a lifestyle that brings happiness and fulfillment.

> **For there will be no prospect for the evil man; the lamp of the wicked will be put out.**
>
> **—Proverbs 24:20**

Overwork Is Not Acceptable

Overdoing will ruin your marriage. If you become a willing slave to your job, it will devastate your family. Work, love, rest, exercise, play, worship, meals, and social contacts must be carefully balanced in your marriage, or something will snap. Overwork and the lack of sleep make a person critical, intolerant, and negative. Constant bickering is a great evil that dulls one's principles.

Overworking is nothing new. It existed in times past and still exists today. Unless the Lord builds a house, then the builder labors in vain. All the toiling and hard work is of no purpose unless they are for the purpose that God has given you. Do not overwork and forget about the blessing that God has given you — your family!

Work according to what God has called you to do, in moderation, and you will find contentment!

Overwork is not acceptable in the life of the Believer and must be avoided in order to build a lifestyle that brings happiness and fulfillment.

> **It is vain for you to rise up early, to sit up late, to eat the bread of sorrows; for so He gives His beloved sleep.**
>
> **—Psalm 127:2**

God Encourages Savings, but He Abhors Hoarding

The question is not; "Do I save or do I give." Giving and saving should be practiced at the same time!

1. Earn as much as you can without neglecting your other responsibilities.
2. Give generously all the time. Give sacrificially, without hesitation, when the Lord leads you to do so.
3. Save the rest. God frequently provides what we need ahead of time. Save for those unexpected circumstances that will certainly arise in your life.

When you begin to examine your saving, spending, and hoarding tendencies, you will really be examining your heart. Jesus said that where our money (treasure) is, there our heart would also be. Both our hearts and our finances need to be right before the Lord. Sometimes we must simply take a step of faith and get our finances right so that our heart will begin to follow! Think about it. Is that not exactly what Jesus said?

Those who save and do not give demonstrate characteristics of a hoarder. Saving in excess is a sign of greed as well as a lack of trust in the Lord. It also displays a love of money.

Do you squander your income?

Do you save regularly and give regularly?

Do you hoard the money that comes into your hands?

The one who squanders lacks self-control, the one who saves and gives has self-control, the one who hoards has greed.

Each family must prayerfully find the right balance. Wasteful spending does not honor God; accumulating massive amounts of money dishonors God, too. We must find the right balance between spending, saving, and giving in order to please God in our finances.

Hoarding is not acceptable in the life of the Believer and must be avoided in order to build a lifestyle that brings happiness and fulfillment.

Saving and giving honors God and will help build a lifestyle that brings happiness and fulfillment.

> There is desirable treasure, and oil in the dwelling of the wise, but a foolish man squanders it.
>
> —Proverbs 21:20

> For this you know, that no fornicator, unclean person, nor covetous man, who is an idolater, has any inheritance in the kingdom of Christ and God.
>
> —Ephesians 5:5

You Cannot Protect Your Family, but God Can!

Throughout the Bible, God invites us to call upon Him. You and your spouse must become a couple who gives emphasis to prayer and seeking God. Distraction, anxieties, burdens, and worries— learn to cast them all upon the Lord.

Calling on God in times of trouble brings glory to God. It is recognition that God is the One who is in control. When you call on God in the day of trouble, it demonstrates that you possess a genuine and sincere belief in God's existence, in His power, and in His incessant care of His people. It speaks of your confidence in the great "I AM" that is far beyond the mere lip service of those who vainly repeat the same prayers day in and day out. Calling upon God honors His goodness and acknowledges His faithfulness.

Surely the Lord knows best what pleases Him, and if He declares that He delights in our calling upon Him in the day of trouble, why should we dispute with Him?

It is a blessed thing when we can say, "Though He slay me, yet will I trust in Him." When we say that with our words or our thoughts, it then brings glory to God when His answer is, "I will deliver thee."

You cannot protect your family, but when you call upon God, He will help you to build a lifestyle that brings happiness and fulfillment.

> **Offer to God thanksgiving, and pay your vows to the Most High. Call upon Me in the day of trouble; I will deliver you, and you shall glorify Me.**
>
> **—Psalms 50:14-15**

Balance

Provision for your family's needs is God's standard. The principle here is balance. God expects us to work to provide for the needs of our family. Nevertheless, He expects us to know when to stop working and go home! That is balance. Do not overwork to be rich. Cease! Look around and you can see its negative effect in many families. Do not do it!

Believe God

God may provide differently than you expect, but He will undoubtedly provide more of Himself when you seek Him. His ultimate provision has already been given to you through the Gospel and it is that provision that provides for eternity.

Believe God's promise that your needs will be met! Sometimes He will provide through an abundance of resources. Other times He will provide for you in your lack. God frequently provides in our lack through the generosity of other Believers. However He chooses to provide, accept it. It is part of his perfect plan for your life. Learn to be content.

God *Always* Keeps His Promises

When trouble comes, you must rest in the certainty that Jesus has promised that He will never leave you nor forsake you.

God always keeps His promises. People will fail, even when they are sincere. People forget, but God cannot forget. God never forgets! The only thing that God forgets is our sins! He has thrown them into the deepest sea!

God will provide and He will help you to build a lifestyle that brings happiness and fulfillment.

> Let your conduct be without covetousness; be content with such things as you have. For He Himself has said, "I WILL NEVER LEAVE YOU NOR FORSAKE YOU."
>
> —Hebrews 13:5

So, how much cash should you have on hand for current needs? It will vary greatly depending on your family and its needs. Nevertheless, it will include enough to meet current obligations plus a reasonable amount of short-term cash reserves. If you fail to make provision to meet the current needs, your family will suffer as a result.

How Much Do You Need for Investments?

God has given some people the gift of giving. Many of these people will be effective at investing and making money. It is important to be careful to not fall into the trap of reinvesting all the profits. That will quickly lead to hoarding. Always give God the tithes out of the first fruits of the increase. Give generously as the Lord leads, and then invest the remainder in order to have more to give.

Do you remember the parable of the talents in Luke 19:11-26? God does call some to be investors! Nevertheless, He does expect that they will make wise investments that will yield the best results and that they use the proceeds from their investments well.

It is God who calls the investor in order to provide for the Kingdom and His people. The investor must be willing to reinvest in the work of the Lord. It is through investments that God supplies a surplus for the church, missions, and the needs of the saints. However, if you allow yourself to think that you are doing it, instead of the Lord, it will bring about pride and loss.

> Now the multitude of those who believed were of one heart and one soul; neither did anyone say

that any of the things he possessed was his own,
but they had all things in common. And with great
power the apostles gave witness to the resurrec-
tion of the Lord Jesus. And great grace was upon
them all. Nor was there anyone among them who
lacked; for all who were possessors of lands or
houses sold them, and brought the proceeds of
the things that were sold, and laid them at the
apostles' feet; and they distributed to each as anyone had need.

—Acts 4:32-35

For those who are called to invest, Larry Burkett gives these simple guidelines to follow.

- Stay with what you know.
- Do not risk borrowed money.
- Buy assets with utility.
- Seek godly counsel.
- Ask the Lord and wait upon His reply.
- If you do not have peace … stop.
- How much do you need for retirement?

The mindset of the world and, unfortunately, the church, began to change dramatically in August 14, 1935, when the Social Security Act was enacted in the United States.

The Bible does not ever talk about retirement! There is never a time in the life of a healthy Believer that one should stop working. Your work on earth should not end until the day you die. While it is true that your work may change as you get older, your work does not stop! The concept most people have of retirement is not a Biblical concept.

When you focus on retirement, then you give little attention to God's plan for your life and your resources. Yes, you should have long-term savings for your latter years when income decreases due to the changes in your work, but the idea of setting aside thousands or hundreds of thousands of dollars for retirement is a farce. Instead of giving to the Lord's work and His people, as you should, you are setting your children up in a situation where they will be tempted to fight over your excess wealth.

Plan toward the less productive years in which your income will likely decrease. That is wisdom. Do not develop the attitude of hoarding. Leave an inheritance to your children that will be passed on to their children—the gift of giving into the Lord's work.

> As for every man to whom God has given riches and wealth, and given him power to eat of it, to receive his heritage and rejoice in his labor—this is the gift of God. For he will not dwell unduly on the days of his life, because God keeps him busy with the joy of his heart.
>
> —Ecclesiastes 5:19-20

God promises to provide all that you need if you will seek Him first, and that includes finances. If you will seek God throughout your life, He will preserve you in your latter years.

> For all these things the nations of the world seek after, and your Father knows that you need these things. But seek the kingdom of God, and all these things shall be added to you.
>
> —Luke 12:30-31

> For the LORD loves justice, and does not forsake His saints; they are preserved forever, but the descendants of the wicked shall be cut off.
>
> —Psalm 37:28

How Much Should You Leave for an Inheritance?

God has clearly called all Believers to provide for their families, but He has not called us to profit them upon our death through excessive insurance. People somehow believe that large sums of money will protect their families upon their deaths, but take a moment to reread Luke 15:11-24, the story of the prodigal son. It shows clearly the results of providing excess funds to your children through inheritance.

I am not saying do not leave anything to your children or your children's children. Before you decide on the proper amount, ask yourself, will this cause my kids to covet or prevent them from earning their own way in life, or will it help them provide reasonably for their family and encourage them to share?

> But if anyone does not provide for his own, and especially for those of his household, he has denied the faith and is worse than an unbeliever.

> —1 Timothy 5:8

Your inheritance should provide for your family, not try to protect them from all uncertainties. A joy is born in your children when they learn to provide for themselves.

> I have coveted no one's silver or gold or apparel. Yes, you yourselves know that these hands have provided for my necessities, and for those who were with me. I have shown you in every way, by laboring like this, that you must support the weak. And remember the words of the Lord Jesus, that He said, 'It is more blessed to give than to receive.'"

> —Acts 20:33-35

Whatever you do, do not let an inheritance become a stumbling block for your children.

> Then He said to another, "Follow Me." But he said, "Lord, let me first go and bury my father."

> —Luke 9:59

Chapter 11

What Does the LORD Require of Me?

Let's begin considering tithes and offerings by reviewing briefly their purposes and uses.

The primary purpose is to obey God's command. We should give regularly and proportionally.

We also need to realize that it is through giving that the local church flourishes. This not only includes the maintenance needs of the building or other facilities belonging to the church, but also to help its members when there are exceptional needs within the body. Funds are for helping the widow, fulfilling the requirements of 1 Timothy 5. They are also for blessing those who minister among us. This is a concept mentioned in the Old Testament, as well as in the New Testament.

> Behold, I have given the children of Levi all the
> tithes in Israel as an inheritance in return for the

> work which they perform, the work of the taber-
> nacle of meeting.

> —Numbers 18:21

> Let the elders who rule well be counted worthy of
> double honor, especially those who labor in the
> word and doctrine. For the Scripture says, "You
> shall not muzzle an ox while it treads out the
> grain," and, "The laborer is worthy of his wages."

> —1 Timothy 5:17-18

The first time that I taught about this subject in my church in Mexico, I refused to receive offerings, saying that I did not have a need. Since the Bible says, "It is more blessed to give than to receive," I believe I made a serious error in judgment and hampered the possibility of an even greater blessing upon my church and its people.

It is important to note that nobody is exempt from being faithful in giving tithes and offerings. Even those who live from the tithes have the responsibility for being faithful in that area.

> Speak thus to the Levites, and say to them: "When
> you take from the children of Israel the tithes
> which I have given you from them as your inher-
> itance, then you shall offer up a heave offering of
> it to the LORD, a tenth of the tithe."

> —Numbers 18:26

During a trip to the United States, we heard a young woman named Jayme Farris tell about the work that the Lord was doing with orphans in Romania. Upon our return to Mexico, we told the Believers in Baratillo about the work.

Jayme, as a nineteen-year-old, had spent a year in Romania. During that time, she met a woman who was running an orphanage for abandoned babies out of her small apartment. The Lord put a burden on Jayme's heart to buy property and fund a building for this orphanage. She returned home and began to try to fulfill that vision.

When Pam and I shared Jayme's vision with our church in Baratillo, their hearts were touched. The following week, the people in the church decided that they would like to help with the work at the orphanage.

I cried when I realized the significance of the sacrifice that they made to help advance the work in Romania. One man gave over two week's income. Then Sunday, his wife said she wanted to have a part in it too so she gave another one hundred pesos. All the people in the church were new Believers, yet every one of them chose to help the work in Romania. It is their prayer, as well as mine, that God will bless that work.

Tithes and offerings support the work of reaching the world for Christ and the advancement of the Kingdom of God. It is precisely for this reason that our church is supporting missions in Africa, Romania, and Chihuahua, Mexico. They are the means of expressing our love for Christ and His church.

How consistent have you been in your offerings to God? Are you tithing and giving regularly to God? If not, you are being disobedient. Remember, the tithe is a minimum amount. Do not fear to give more! Let us be honest with God's tithes.

Tithing: Why Is It Important?

At first glance, the topic of tithes seems to be of little importance for the family. However, it is a topic of utmost importance. Yet it is a subject that many pastors rarely cover in detail. Why is it that many Believers react poorly to the topic of tithes?

> "For I am the LORD, I do not change; Therefore you are not consumed, O sons of Jacob. Yet from the days of your fathers You have gone away from My ordinances and have not kept them. Return to Me, and I will return to you," says the LORD of hosts. "But you said, 'In what way shall we return?' Will a man rob God? Yet you have robbed Me! But you say, 'In what way have we robbed You?' In tithes and offerings. You are cursed with a curse, for you have robbed Me, Even this whole nation. Bring all the tithes into the storehouse, that there may be food in My house, and try Me now in this," says the LORD of hosts, "if I will not

open for you the windows of heaven and pour out
for you such blessing That there will not be room
enough to receive it. And I will rebuke the de-
vourer for your sakes, so that he will not destroy
the fruit of your ground, nor shall the vine fail to
bear fruit for you in the field," says the LORD of
hosts; "And all nations will call you blessed, for
you will be a delightful land," says the LORD of
hosts. "Your words have been harsh against Me,"
says the LORD, "yet you say, 'What have we spoken against You?' You have said, 'It is useless to
serve God; What profit is it that we have kept His
ordinance, and that we have walked as mourners
Before the LORD of hosts?'"

—Malachi 3:6-14

Malachi is not talking about the tithe, but dishonesty towards
God. Honesty is a major problem for all human beings, including
Believers. Malachi places tithing in the wider context of repentance
and turning back to God.

Notice that, before entering into the topic of tithes and offerings,
God pronounces a declaration of an inflexible judgment against the
people in Malachi 3:5.

"And I will come near you for judgment; I will be
a swift witness against sorcerers, against adulter-
ers, against perjurers, against those who exploit
wage earners and widows and orphans, and
against those who turn away an alien—because
they do not fear Me," says the LORD of hosts.

—Malachi 3:5

The dishonesty of the people towards God was reprehensible
before the eyes of the Lord. The people were behaving as practical
atheists, veiled with an appearance of piety and spirituality. They
had been dishonest in submitting their tithes and offerings. This
dishonesty is what we are dealing with. I pray that you will listen
to this subject with a heart and mind willing to listen to the voice of
God. May it be the Spirit who brings clarity to your minds and

honesty to your hearts. This subject has become a difficult matter on which to teach and meditate for several reasons.

Why do Believers react harshly to the topic of tithes? For some reason that I cannot explain, money is linked to our spiritual lives — just as it is linked to our devotional lives, our conduct, and everything we do with our bodies. If the subject of tithes and offerings were not relevant to our spiritual lives, then the prophet would not have placed it in the context of a call to repentance and a return to God. A fundamental truth regarding faithfulness and honesty in stewardship is that both are always considered the fruit from repentance and an indication of a deep commitment to God.

The results of a recent survey say a lot regarding the condition of the church. It was found that 17% of the members of the church say that they tithe, but really only 3% truly tithe. That is, 14% say that they tithe, but really do not. They are not being honest with God, the church, or their brethren. They are also not being honest with themselves. What this means is that 83% admit they do not tithe but, in reality, 97% of Believers are not obeying God in the area of tithes and offerings.

> Will a man rob God? Yet you have robbed Me!
> But you say, 'In what way have we robbed You?'
> In tithes and offerings.
>
> —Malachi 3:8

Tithing has also become a difficult topic to speak about effectively. Many of my readers know me and should be able to evaluate my motives as I deal strongly with this subject. It is time that we change our distorted perspectives regarding money.

The tithes, as well as offerings, are based on three fundamental truths for the Christian life: repentance, faith, and commitment to God. These three truths place the practice of tithing at the level it belongs: in worship. That is why the confrontation in Malachi 1:6 begins with the following words: "'A son honors his father and a servant his master. If then I am the Father, where is my honor? And if I am a Master, where is my reverence?' says the LORD of hosts to you priests who despise My name. 'Yet you say, "In what way have we despised your name"'"?

Tithes and offerings are part of your worship of God, just as are your singing, praying, and commitment of your life to God. The tithe is laid aside, the offerings are consecrated, and both are brought and presented to God as an act of worship, together with your very life. That is the principle expressed in Romans 12:1.

> **I beseech you therefore, brethren, by the mercies of God, that you present your bodies a living sacrifice, holy, acceptable to God, which is your reasonable service.**
>
> —Romans 12:1

In Malachi, God is once again extending an invitation of grace for the people to turn back to Him—in tithes and offerings. God makes the accusation that the people have robbed Him. Rob means to cheat or defraud someone. For most people, robbery is bad enough, but robbing God is unthinkable. In Malachi, the worshipers had kept for themselves part of the tithes and offerings, and were using them for their own benefit. That was dishonest. The main purpose of tithes and offerings is that they are consecrated to the Lord's service.

Jesus said, "God is Spirit, and those who worship Him must worship in spirit and truth" (John 4:24). With their words the people were worshiping and proclaiming God as their Father, King and Lord. But by withholding part of the tithes and offerings, they were renouncing God's sovereignty and authority. Likewise, if we sing "Jesus Is My Sovereign King" but withhold part of the tithes and offerings, then we are also renouncing God's sovereignty and authority.

The tithes and offerings are not a tip we give to God for services rendered. Neither are they a fee we pay to keep His blessings coming. Did you know that giving our tithes and offerings implies that God is the owner of everything? For this reason, worship by means of tithes and offerings must be in the Spirit. It should be in truth because truth is the character of God.

Negligent stewardship is equivalent to fraud. When this happens, worship passes from true to false and the question arises, "In what way have we robbed you?" God pronounces over them a "curse with a curse."

In Galatians 6:7 the Bible says, "Do not be deceived, God is not mocked; for whatever a man sows, that he will also reap." I am not invoking judgment, nor a curse, on my readers, but I do want to say that all those who withhold for themselves, partially or totally, what belongs to God will find out that they will never be able to enjoy it and will only see it vanish. Just like Ananias and Sapphira, we will lose what we think we have stored for ourselves.

God did not leave matters there; He challenged the people to do what was right: "Bring all the tithes into the storehouse"; to be responsible: "that there may be food in my house"; and to trust completely in Him. This is the only place in the Bible where God says, "Try Me now in this!" The Lord God Almighty is saying, "Try me now in this. If I will not open for you the windows of heaven and pour out for you such blessing that there will not be room enough to receive it."

Honesty is what God needs to hear and see in the actions of His people. Jesus said, "But why do you call me 'Lord, Lord,' and not do the things which I say?"

If tithes and offerings were not relevant to our spiritual life, then God would not have placed them in the context of a call to repentance and a turning back to God with a promise. Since it is an act of worship, it should be practiced with dignity. Our dignity is a sign of respect towards God and His commandments. "'For I am a great King,' says the LORD of hosts, 'And My name is to be feared among the nations'" (Malachi 1:14). If you want God's blessing, be honest with Him and with yourself!

It does not have to do with quantity but with quality—with the condition and disposition of the heart. God is not so much interested in what you give, but in how you give it. He says He loves a cheerful giver; therefore, He sees with disdain those who give grudgingly, grumbling or miserly. If we give for the cause of God, even if we do not seem to have enough, it can only mean one thing: we trust that God will provide.

If you find yourself in the situation where you are not tithing, nor giving offerings as God teaches, what should you do? First, you should repent and begin to do what is right. Ask the Lord, what is it that You require of me?

> "Bring all the tithes into the storehouse, that there may be food in My house, and try Me now in this," says the LORD of hosts, "if I will not open for you the windows of heaven and pour out for you such blessing that there will not be room enough to receive it."

> —Malachi 3:10

Tithes Are Your Test

I want to teach you a spiritual principle that will bring blessing to your house and your life. It will help you see in a deeper way what is involved in bringing to God our tithes and offerings.

Cain brought an offering to God from the fruit of the ground. Abel also brought an offering, but from the firstborn of his sheep, from the fattest of them. The Lord had regard for Abel and his offering; but for Cain and his offering, he had no regard. Cain was very angry, so the Lord said to Cain, "Why are you angry? Why has your countenance fallen? If you do well, will you not be accepted? And if you do not do well, sin lies at the door" (Genesis 4:6-7).

God initiated the system of tithes and offerings; therefore, it is unique and must be carried out responsibly and with understanding. Offerings are gifts presented to God. Tithes are your test.

In this story, we see two brothers bringing their offerings to the Lord, but there is a difference between them. Abel presented his offering in a manner that God approved, while Cain brought his offering in a manner that was convenient for him. God was pleased with one, but with the other, He was not pleased. Why? God does not look at quantities, but He sees the heart of man.

Our tithes and offerings are visible indicators for expressing obedience; that is, for paying attention to God's will and acting accordingly to fulfill it. Obedience to God requires a total commitment to His will. Obedience and faith are intimately related.

Worship is part of your reasonable service, of your way of honoring and respecting God. Devotion is a boundless manifestation of love towards God. Your promptness to obey Him is a manifestation of your obedience. Our tithes and offerings are an expression of thanksgiving for what He has done and for what He will do. Tithes and offerings demonstrate your relationship to God.

Are you upright before Him?

Do you have a right relationship with Him?

Our tithes and offerings show our commitment to God.

Do you trust God wholeheartedly? Do you think He is not capable of taking care of you?

Bringing your tithes and offerings should be an act born from your heart. God did not establish them to be a nuisance or an oppression to us but to bless us; and since this command is part of His will, it is good, acceptable, and perfect.

> Speak to the children of Israel, that they bring Me
> an offering. From everyone who gives it willingly
> with his heart you shall take My offering.
>
> —Exodus 25:2

Many times, as stewards of the finances that God has given us, we act like Cain, taking tithes and offerings as something trivial. Then when we go through trials, we get upset with God, when, in reality, it is ourselves who are bringing those consequences to our homes.

The LORD said to Cain, "If you do well, will you not be accepted? And if you do not do well, sin lies at the door, in wait" (Genesis 4:6-7). What is important to God is not how much you give, but that you give in a right away. That is why He has determined that your tithe be 10% and your offerings be according to how He has blessed you. God does not ask us for something if He has not first moved to supply it. God's desire is to bless you; He is just waiting for you to allow Him to do so by doing His will.

According to the Bible, each person should establish their own offering plan, and then give it cheerfully.

> Honor the LORD with your possessions, And with
> the first fruits of all your increase.
>
> —Proverbs 3:9

Honor God

If we honor the Lord with our finances, we do so when we give Him our tithes and offerings. That is only the beginning. We must also honor Him with our time, our efforts, our words, and definitely with our own lives.

> Now may He who supplies seed to the sower,
> and bread for food, supply and multiply the
> seed you have sown and increase the fruits of
> your righteousness, while you are enriched in
> everything for all liberality, which causes

thanksgiving through us to God. For the administration of this service not only supplies the needs of the saints, but also is abounding through many thanksgivings to God, while, through the proof of this ministry, they glorify God for the obedience of your confession to the gospel of Christ, and for your liberal sharing with them and all men, and by their prayer for you, who long for you because of the exceeding grace of God in you. Thanks be to God for His indescribable gift!

—2 Corinthians 9:10-15

What do we learn about giving from this text?

Giving is a great personal benefit—"He who sows bountifully will also reap bountifully." The act of giving pleases the Lord—"For God loves a cheerful giver." Giving expresses our trust in God—"And God is able to make all grace abound to you." Giving causes expressions of thanksgiving to be made to God—"Overflowing in many thanksgivings to God." It gives us assurance in our relationship with Christ and advances the preaching of the gospel—"For the obedience of your confession to the gospel of Christ."

Fill My Cup!

Once when I was in the United States, I attended a conference. During the conference, there was a special class for the children. The focus of that class was missions. The teachers, trying to teach the concept of giving, gave each child a container to collect money for missions. The children went around asking people for money, mainly coins, to fill their container.

What is the problem with collecting money in this fashion?

Firstly, the children were not giving from their own funds or resources; they were going around "begging" for money for God. Secondly, they were doing it publicly so that everyone could see how much money they were collecting.

In Deuteronomy God commanded the Israelites to give Him the tenth of their harvests. We call this tithing—ten percent of all the profits we make.

> You shall truly tithe all the increase of your grain
> that the field produces year by year.
>
> —Deuteronomy 14:22

When the Israelites were giving their tithes to God, God blessed them, but when they were not tithing, God said they were robbing Him.

> "Will a man rob God? Yet you have robbed
> Me! But you say, 'In what way have we robbed
> You?' In tithes and offerings. You are cursed
> with a curse, for you have robbed Me, even
> this whole nation. Bring all the tithes into the
> storehouse, that there may be food in My
> house, and try Me now in this," says the LORD
> of hosts, "if I will not open for you the windows
> of heaven and pour out for you such blessing
> that there will not be room enough to receive
> it."
>
> —Malachi 3:8-10

Thus, what shall we do with the riches God gives us?

> Honor the LORD with your possessions, and with
> the first fruits of all your increase; so your barns
> will be filled with plenty, and your vats will over-
> flow with new wine.
>
> —Proverbs 3:9-10

> Every man shall give as he is able, according to
> the blessing of the LORD your God which He has
> given you.
>
> —Deuteronomy 16:17

Then each one should give from the first fruits of all his profits according to God's blessing.

10% and 90% for Me!

Nowadays, there are Christians who tithe and, with that, they believe they have fulfilled their duties before God. If they have made one hundred dollars, they set apart ten to put in the offering. If they have made one thousand dollars, they set apart one hundred to put in the offering—the tithe belongs to God; the other ninety percent belongs to them.

Is this true? NO.

The New Testament teaches that we should surrender all our heart to God. We must say, "Lord, all I have belongs to you. If you ask me to give it to someone else, I will give it to him."

We must seek first the Kingdom of God. In other words, we must surrender to God all our heart and all we have.

A young, rich man came to Jesus and asked Him what he should do to have eternal life.

> Now behold, one came and said to Him, "Good Teacher, what good thing shall I do that I may have eternal life?" So He said to him, "Why do you call Me good? No one is good but One, that is, God. But if you want to enter into life, keep the commandments." He said to Him, "Which ones?" Jesus said, "'You shall not murder,' 'you shall not commit adultery,' 'you shall not steal,' 'you shall not bear false witness,' 'honor your father and your mother,' and, 'you shall love your neighbor as yourself.'" The young man said to Him, "All these things I have kept from my youth. What do I still lack?" Jesus said to him, "If you want to be perfect, go, sell what you have and give to the poor, and you will have treasure in heaven; and come, follow Me." But when the young man heard that saying, he went away sorrowful, for he had great possessions.
>
> —Matthew 19:16-22

Jesus told him to sell all he had and to give it to the poor. The rich man did not want to sell what he had. Why? Because he had not surrendered his heart to God. His heart was glued to his possessions.

When we surrender our heart to God, our heart is glued to spiritual things—to heavenly things. For this reason, we must think of our possessions as things that belong to God. If we have this attitude—our possessions belong to God—we will be willing to share with others what we have. That is how we make treasures in heaven.

How Should I Give?

Let us now look at how we should give our offerings.

> And He looked up and saw the rich putting their gifts into the treasury, and He saw also a certain poor widow putting in two mites. So He said, "Truly I say to you that this poor widow has put in more than all; for all these out of their abundance have put in offerings for God, but she out of her poverty put in all the livelihood that she had."
>
> —Luke 21:1-4

> Take heed that you do not do your charitable deeds before men, to be seen by them. Otherwise you have no reward from your Father in heaven. Therefore, when you do a charitable deed, do not sound a trumpet before you as the hypocrites do in the synagogues and in the streets, that they may have glory from men. Assuredly, I say to you, they have their reward. But when you do a charitable deed, do not let your left hand know what your right hand is doing, that your charitable deed may be in secret; and your Father who sees in secret will Himself reward you openly.
>
> —Matthew 6:1-4

We should give cheerfully as an expression of appreciation.

> So let each one give as he purposes in his heart,
> not grudgingly or of necessity; for God loves a
> cheerful giver.

>   —2 Corinthians 9:7

We give in order to receive God's blessing. We give because we know God has promised to bless those who give.

> But this I say: He who sows sparingly will also
> reap sparingly, and he who sows bountifully will
> also reap bountifully.

>   —2 Corinthians 9:6

Maybe here on earth we will never know the impact of our contributions to the Kingdom of God, but we wait eagerly for Heaven with the expectation to see the lives that were changed through our generosity and listen to our Heavenly Father say, "Well done, good and faithful servant." That is why we give generously. Therefore, we should not only give from our surplus but we should also give sacrificially. We should not give so man can see what we do, but we should give in secret whenever we can. Moreover, what is most important is that we should give cheerfully in our hearts. It is good to ask ourselves occasionally: Do I give offerings because I am in the habit of doing so? Do I give offerings in order to impress my brother? Do I give offerings because I love the Lord?

God wants us to give offerings. He loves the cheerful giver. It is true that we give in secret, but God knows!

The People Bring Much More Than Needed!

We can learn from the example of Moses and the Israelites. Moses was not going around looking for offerings outside of God's people; he took offerings only from among God's people.

> Take from among you an offering to the LORD.
> Whoever is of a willing heart, let him bring it as
> an offering to the LORD: gold, silver, and bronze.

>   —Exodus 35:5

The people gave cheerfully.

> Then Moses called Bezalel and Aholiab, and every
> gifted artisan in whose heart the LORD had put wis-
> dom, everyone whose heart was stirred, to come
> and do the work. And they received from Moses all
> the offering which the children of Israel had brought
> for the work of the service of making the sanctuary.
> So they continued bringing to him freewill offerings
> every morning. Then all the craftsmen who were do-
> ing all the work of the sanctuary came, each from the
> work he was doing, and they spoke to Moses, say-
> ing, "The people bring much more than enough for
> the service of the work which the LORD commanded
> us to do." So Moses gave a commandment, and they
> caused it to be proclaimed throughout the camp,
> saying, "Let neither man nor woman do any more
> work for the offering of the sanctuary." And the peo-
> ple were restrained from bringing, for the material
> they had was sufficient for all the work to be done—
> indeed too much.
>
> —Exodus 36:2-7

Then Moses ceased the offerings of the people. He commanded that no one should continue to bring offerings for the sanctuary because the people had already provided all that was needed. God loves the cheerful giver.

Why Is It So Hard to Give?

If people were honest, most would recognize that they are used to thinking first about themselves, then about "me," and finally about "myself." A Biblical principle says, "It is more blessed to give than to receive"; however, reality proves that, for most of us, we think that it is better to receive than to give; it is hard to be generous. When it has to do with supplying needs, it is easy for us to justify our selfishness, because we have a lot of "needs." Why seek to help someone else when our family has many needs?

God's Word clearly states that it is better to give than to receive. The truth is that powerful things happen when we decide to take our focus away from our own needs, and even greater miracles occur when we decide to give in spite of our own needs.

God's Character

Our goal is to have God's character. That is, to restore His image in me—and God is generous.

- He gave us His only begotten Son.
- He gave us the Comforter.
- He gives us the keys to the Kingdom of Heaven.
- He gives us living water.
- He gives us eternal life.
- He gives us an inheritance.
- He gives us son-ship.

God did not focus on Himself. He gave us everything—without conditions. When we practice giving, we enable miracles to move in our environment. You may be the miracle someone is waiting for. As long as you are focusing on yourself, you miss the opportunity to be a blessing to others.

How Much Do You Need?

You must determine how much money you need to live on, and then do not keep more than that amount because that will only bring sorrow to you. Determine how much you need for your everyday living and what you need in reserves. For this, we have the example of the ant. Ants work hard and are very creative. With what appears to be little effort, they can gain access to nearly all food sources.

One day, I walked out of my house and saw what appeared to be a piece of grated cheese walking across the yard! I stopped in my tracks and began to examine it. There was a tiny ant carrying it. The cheese was four times the size of the ant. As he walked, he looked like he stopped to communicate with the other ants, and then he continued on his journey. After walking about three yards, he arrived at his anthill. Many other ants joined him in breaking down the cheese to take it underground for storage.

God tells us to go to the ant and learn his ways. The ants' way is the way of wisdom. They work hard, they work together, and they look for creative ways to complete a task.

That reminds me of something that happened when my children were young. We had developed a problem with ants in our log cabin. They seemed to be everywhere and showed up at many unwanted places.

Large red ants had taken up residence around the sink in the bathroom. Little black ones showed up in the kitchen anytime food was accidentally left on the counter. Then there were the mid-size black ones that tended to show up anytime and everywhere.

One week, the kids got up early in the morning and asked for hot chocolate. While Pam was preparing breakfast, Joshua heated the milk and then finished preparing the hot chocolate.

After breakfast was ready, Pam gave everyone a nice warm cup of hot chocolate, topped with some fresh mini marshmallows. The warm, rich chocolate quickly melted the marshmallows, leaving a puffy mass of velvety white marshmallow cream floating in the top of the cup.

As Isaac was lifting his cup to his mouth, he suddenly set it down and exclaimed, "I have a piece of protein in my cup—an ant!" When he asked for a spoon to get it out, Benjamin quickly offered the use of his spoon. Then he hurriedly added, "Give it back with the ant."

Once Isaac retrieved the ant, he held the spoon out to Benjamin. Benjamin grabbed the spoon with great enthusiasm and examined the ant. Then, without saying anything, he opened his mouth and quickly ate the ant before anyone could get the words, "Don't eat that!" out of their mouth.

With six kids sitting around the table, a roar of laughter followed. Embarrassed by the laughter, he shyly turned his head and hid his face.

While we are always looking for creative ways to reduce expenses, we hoped that this did not establish a new eating pattern.

You probably do not want to start eating ants to reduce your food bill, but you could learn from them! Their way is the way to wisdom. Learn to work hard, work as a team, and look for creative ways to complete a task.

As Soon as You Receive More Money Than You Need, Get Rid of It!

No, I am not crazy. Otherwise, you will be laying up treasures for yourself, and the Lord forbids that. He forbids it just as He forbids murder and adultery. Every dollar you accumulate in excess of what you really need will be robbing you from your treasures in heaven—because you are not giving it for the cause of Christ. Do not invest your excess funds in an earthly bank! It is better to invest your funds to promote the cause of Christ here on earth, then you will have great treasures in heaven.

Why spend money on what is not profitable when you could spend it on something God would reward?

Our motto should be: Earn as much as you can, save as much as you can, and give as much as you can. God anointed us to give! God will always multiply the fruit of what you sow.

> "Bring the full tithe into the storehouse, that there may be food in my house. And thereby put me to the test," says the LORD of hosts, "if I will not open the windows of heaven for you and pour down for you a blessing until there is no more need."
>
> —Malachi 3:10

Note from the author: I am grateful to all the pastors who have shared their studies on this topic with me. I am especially grateful to Pastor Fernando Ocampo, who first shared the idea of dishonesty towards God with me, and for his willingness to allow me to use that material in this chapter.

Chapter 12

Giving

In the last chapter, we focused on the tithe—giving 10% as God has specifically directed. The tithe not only establishes our recognition of the fact that God is the true owner of all that we have in our possession, but is also a living testimony of that fact. Once you firmly establish the principle of God's ownership, in your mind and in your actions, the next level of giving opens up to you—the joy of giving gifts.

God will begin to reveal needs of those around you and help you to recognize a responsibility to meet them. Those needs will often vary greatly from person to person. God will call some to help with physical needs, He will call others to help with material needs, and He will call others to help meet the needs of the missionaries and other Christian ministries.

Larry Burkett described God's plan for giving this way:

God's plan for sharing begins with:

- Tithe—a testimony to God's ownership
- Obedience—helping the obvious needs around us
- Abundance—giving from our surplus
- Sacrifice—yielding our wants and needs for others

On the Road Again

Others have blessed our lives abundantly. A few years ago, we set out on a trip to visit family in the United States. Following that trip, we had many stories to tell about God's faithfulness and how He uses the hands of Believers to bless and meet needs.

As we left Mexico, we asked for God's protection while we were traveling. Little did we know that He would provide an abundance of opportunities to show us His protection.

When we began our trip, the air conditioner was not working properly, so we sweated our way from Mexico to Georgia (via Texas, Tennessee and Virginia). In Georgia, a mechanic asked me if we were having any problems with the van. I told him no, because we had gotten used to the heat and I had forgotten about the air conditioner. Then he asked me specifically if the air conditioner was working okay. I told him that it was not getting cold. That week he came to where we were staying and put some Freon "stop leak" in the system, then filled it up with Freon. He even replaced a burnt-out head light.

While we were in Covington, Georgia a few days later, the air conditioner was getting warm again. The man we were staying with just happened to be an air conditioner mechanic. He replaced the seals, valve stems, and Freon. While he was doing that work, he noticed the fan belts were worn so he replaced them. While he was replacing those, he saw a large crack in the radiator fan so he replaced that as well. All of this work was done without any charge and we were back on the road again.

Two days later, I was driving down the freeway and the car over heated. The radiator had a small leak in the seam. When we tried to get it repaired, we found out that it was not repairable. The man at the radiator shop asked me where we were from in Texas (the van had Texas tags). When he found out we were missionaries, he gave us a 15% discount. It was fixed in no time and we were back on the road again.

Later that day, the coil wire burned into two pieces and the van died on the side of the street. I located the problem in less than two minutes after I prayed, "Lord, help me!" I just happened to have kept the old coil wire from the last time I tuned up the van. It was in my small toolbox in the back of the van. Once again, it was fixed in no time and we were back on the road again.

After this, all seemed to go well—until we left Florida. We were pulling a small U-Haul trailer. As we began to go up hills, the van slowed down a lot. By the time we got to Louisiana the van would not exceed 30 mph at any time. We stopped in a small town and found out that the catalytic converter was stopped up. The mechanic wanted almost $500.00 to make the repair. We decided to go to the next large city to see if we could get it done cheaper. We slowly drove on.

As we were getting off the exit, the clutch stopped working. It was the hydraulic hose for the clutch. This is a dealer-only item. A Ford dealer was located less than a mile from where we were stopped. They quickly repaired the clutch for us. When I asked about the catalytic converter, the service manager told me they were very expensive at Ford. He gave me the name of a shop a few miles from there that fixed it for $125.00. We were now back on the road again.

After going about 20 miles, we hit a big bump in the road and the trailer came off the hitch. The chains came loose too. The hook on the end of the chain caught on the side of the hitch. The tongue was dragging on the ground and the trailer began fishtailing. It seemed to be going up on one wheel, then the other, and then back again. We cried out to the Lord for help and He gave us wisdom in getting the van and trailer stopped. Nobody and nothing was hurt. We hooked the trailer up and we were again back on the road.

As we were about to cross the border into Mexico, the air went out again. This time it was a melted vacuum line. We got that fixed and were back on the road. The clutch was starting to slip, so we bought a new one and had it replaced in Mexico and now we were back on the road yet again.

Through all of this, the Lord protected us. Nobody was harmed and, with every problem we had, enough money was there to take care of the need, or God provided a mechanic. God is truly faithful to meet our every need. I think the best way to describe it is to say that our van had a variety of problems, but God always had a solution, and that solution usually came as the result of a Believer being open to the prompting of the Holy Spirit.

Giving Is a Byproduct of a Life Committed to Christ.

Our tithes evidence our obedience to God as well as our trust that He will provide for our needs. Giving, beyond the tithes, is a byproduct of a life committed to Christ. We must learn to trust God; we must step out and trust Him even for things that we cannot see.

There are legitimate needs all around us—the poor, single mothers and their children—the elderly who are not being cared for by their families. As Believers, we must come to the point that we are not only willing, but also effective in seeing and meeting these needs. Jesus said, "I was hungry and you gave Me food; I was thirsty and you gave Me drink; I was a stranger and you took Me in; I was naked and you clothed Me; I was sick and you visited Me; I was in prison and you came to Me" (Matthew 25:33-40).

Once again, God has proven that He is wonderful and provides all of our needs.

A Note of Gratitude

We came to the homeschool conference with just enough money for our room and food, having some left over for a few materials. On the way to the conference, our tire went flat. We put on the spare, but it also went flat. We had to buy a new tire, and we no longer had enough money to buy any materials.

When we arrived at the conference, we found a great surprise that the Lord had given us through you. He gives us more than we need.

Thank you very much for letting the Lord guide you. We are sure that God will bless and multiply you.

Jésus and Carmen Garcia

Just Do It!

Sadly, for many people it is more challenging to give out of a surplus than it is to give out of a lack. When people have financial needs in their own life, they tend to be more sensitive to the financial needs of others. When we have an abundance of money, there are many more ways to be tempted to spend it, so the tendency is to overlook the needy.

Do you truly believe that God will let you do without when you sacrificially help someone in need?

If a brother or sister is naked and destitute of daily food, and one of you says to them, "Depart in peace, be warmed and filled," but you do not give them the things which are needed for the body, what does it profit?

—James 2:15-16

Perhaps when Jesus said, "Assuredly, I say to you that it is hard for a rich man to enter the kingdom of heaven," He was thinking about our bank accounts. Frequently, it is easier to give out of our current income than it is to give out of our savings. Once deposited into a savings account, we tend to become possessive—our hearts scream that this is *my* savings! Oh, foolish man, will you not ever learn that God owns it all—even your savings account? We are stewards, not owners. We must make everything, even our surplus, available to God.

There is always sufficient in God's house. Sometimes He gives enough to me for your lack, and sometimes He gives enough to you for my lack, but without a doubt, there is always sufficient in God's house.

As it is written, "He who gathered much had nothing left over, and he who gathered little had no lack."

—2 Corinthians 8:15

A Bed for Lili

Lili was a young single mother with significant physical disabilities when we first arrived in Mexico. She lived with her great-grandparents, along with many other relatives. Their house was very small. Lili and her baby slept on the concrete floor. As Pam began to meet some of her physical needs, Lili opened her heart to the gospel and prayed to accept our Lord.

Lili had some very severe dental problems. We were glad when the Lord provided the funds needed to get her teeth fixed.

Since Lili's daughter was born, the baby had spent her nights sleeping on a concrete floor beside her mother. This was normal since Lili had always slept on the floor too. That changed! The Lord gave her a brand-new rollaway bed. Since her house was very small, she brought the bed out at night but put it away during the day.

She also had many day-to-day struggles. For example, one morning Lili came to our house, along with her baby, at 2:00 a.m. Both were soaking wet from the rain and shivering from the cold. Her uncle had come home drunk and was hitting everyone in sight. When he threw the baby across the room, Lili picked up the child and left the house. In spite of having only known us for a few months, she felt safe coming to our home.

Because of her handicap, Lili did not walk very well. She had been praying, for several months, that God would provide a stroller for her baby. A church in Indiana sent a stroller for us to give to her.

When Pam gave the stroller to Lili, before she opened the box, she read the card they had written. A few minutes later, she was praying and thanking the Lord for His provision. She began to ask God to bless each person who sent it—by name! What a sign of maturing in the Lord, asking God to bless others and not just thinking of herself.

Sacrifice

> For if there is first a willing mind, it is accepted according to what one has, and not according to what he does not have. For I do not mean that others should be eased and you burdened; but by an equality, that now at this time your abundance may supply their lack, that their abundance also may supply your lack—that there may be equality.
>
> —2 Corinthians 8:12-14

Sacrificial giving is a principle that we must teach in the church today. Our tendency is to focus on ourselves instead of others. Everyone has something to give, yet the cares of the world have clouded the minds of many. God calls us to give sacrificially at times. Look around, find someone in need, and be willing to sacrifice. It will help you care for others in the way God desires for you to care for them.

> And He looked up and saw the rich putting their gifts into the treasury, and He saw also a certain poor widow putting in two mites. So He said,

"Truly I say to you that this poor widow has put
in more than all; for all these out of their abundance have put in offerings for God, but she out
of her poverty put in all the livelihood that she
had."

—Luke 21:1-4

But do not forget to do good and to share, for with such sacrifices
God is well pleased.

—Hebrews 13:16

It Is a Bed!

Blanca was a Believer with three children. She lived in a small,
run-down house near a drainage ditch that smelled of sewage.
When I delivered a triple bunk-bed set, one of her boys asked,
"What is it mommy?"
Blanca simply replied, "It is a bed."
It is exciting to see God meet the needs of His people. Ask God
to open your eyes to the needs around you. If you do, you will be
richly blessed when you begin to reach out and help them.

But as you abound in everything—in faith, in
speech, in knowledge, in all diligence, and in
your love for us—see that you abound in this
grace also. I speak not by commandment, but I
am testing the sincerity of your love by the diligence of others. For you know the grace of our
Lord Jesus Christ, that though He was rich, yet for
your sakes He became poor, that you through His
poverty might become rich.

—2 Corinthians 8:7-9

What Would Joaquin Say?

One day, as I was driving home from Saltillo, my mind was
racing from one thought to the other. Finally, I began to concentrate
on the many blessings that the Lord has given to the work here in

Mexico. Having just finished the annual conference in Saltillo, it was, of course, fresh on my mind.

We received many comments about how the conference was a tremendous blessing to those who attended. One person wrote, "The central theme of the conference was very useful to me at this time." Others wrote how God used various sessions to confirm what He was doing in their lives. Many noticed that the new, larger facility made listening and learning much easier.

As I continued down the winding dirt road that cuts through the canyon leading to my house in the mountains, my mind drifted to our church and the Believers in it. As I thought of the men in the church, I felt blessed by their growth in the Lord over the last few years. I named each man in my mind and thought of the many ways that each had shown growth and fruit in their lives.

Finally, I focused in on Don Joaquin. He was one of the first to accept the Lord. He and his wife opened their hearts and allowed the church to meet on their property. At eighty-seven, he was feeble, yet he was constantly trying to improve the shack that we used for the church services. One day when I drove up to his house, he was smiling broadly and said that he had something to show me. He then took me over and showed me my new pulpit. He had taken one of his water drums and given it to me for my pulpit.

Joaquin has gone to be with the Lord now. He was the precious first fruits given to the Lord from our church.

As my mind drifted back to the conference, I wondered what advice Joaquin and his wife, Socorro, would have given to us had they been there. I thought that perhaps they would have said, life is short and soon one of you will be alone—only memories will be left. Take the time to say, "I love you." Do the little niceties that you know your spouse likes. Enjoy each other, love each other, and never go to bed mad because one day, one of you will be alone—only memories will be left. A sweet kiss in the morning costs nothing, saying "I love you" takes little time.

As I continued to think about Joaquin, I began to think about the day that he died. There was crying here on earth because our friend, our brother in Christ, had died, but what about Heaven? There was no crying there! Joaquin heard those sweet words, "Well done, my good and faithful servant."

Joaquin had taken one of his water barrels and given it to me to use as a pulpit. That meant that, when it did not rain, he would have to carry fifty-five more gallons of water than before because he had given his water barrel to me. That was sacrificial giving!

We must understand the concept of sacrificial giving—just as Joaquin understood it. We must stop focusing only on our needs and begin to look out for others. Just like Joaquin, you have something to give! Do not let the cares of this life blind you to the abundant blessing that you have been given or to the needs of others. God has called you to give sacrificially. Find a need and meet it. God will bless you abundantly in this life and in the next—just like Joaquin.

We all love to get things, but many times, we have a hard time being generous. We know that giving blesses those around us, yet many still avoid it. However, not giving will hurt you.

Research has shown that giving improves your health, decreases the risk of dying early[1], and even lowers your blood pressure[2]. Giving is good. The more you give the more it gives back to you.

Giving to others is one of our greatest offerings. When you touch the needy with the gift of love, hearts and lives are changed.

Giving gives back more than you can ever imagine—it gives you the abundant life in Christ.

---

[1] 1999 study led by Doug Oman of the University of California, Berkeley

[2] 2006 study by Rachel Piferi of Johns Hopkins University and Kathleen Lawler of the University of Tennessee

Chapter 13

Whom Should We Help?

If you ask the Lord to open your eyes, you will find that almost everywhere you look there are people with needs. At first, it may seem overwhelming since you cannot help everyone. We must ask God to give us wisdom when deciding whom we should help and whom we should not help. Since wisdom comes from God, we must turn to Him in order determine this.

There are many legitimate needs, and we must be willing to invest our time, talents, and money to help meet them. But there are also many frauds out there too. Instead of helping those who will not help themselves, our focus should be on helping those who *cannot* help themselves.

How Do You Handle Beggars?

When someone on the street asks for money, do you give it to him or do you not give it to him? Sometimes, it can be a tough decision. As a rule, it would be better to offer to buy them some food or a bus ticket. However, there are times that you simply cannot do that. So you must make a decision, sometimes very quickly, to help them or not. Is this a lazy person or is it a true need? Sometimes the decision is not easy to make but, in order to help make that decision, it is important to remember the principles laid down in Scripture. You do not have to support people who refuse to work. "If anyone will not work, neither shall he eat."

You should not help those who are lazy—those who have needs because of their unwillingness to work. In fact, do not have any close associations with the sluggard. Be careful not to learn his ways. Do not be surprised that God has specifically directed you not to help some people! Many times, He is using their challenging times to bring about discipline and correction in their lives. If we interfere in these cases, we are only delaying that discipline and correction. As a result, we are actually making it harder for the person!

> For even when we were with you, we commanded you this: If anyone will not work, neither shall he eat. For we hear that there are some who walk among you in a disorderly manner, not working at all, but are busybodies.
>
> —2 Thessalonians 3:10-11

We should give generously to those whom God has placed on our hearts, but we should avoid becoming trapped by the lies and deceit of the lazy people that refuse to work.

> He who has a generous eye will be blessed, for he gives of his bread to the poor.
>
> —Proverbs 22:9

> Sell what you have and give alms; provide yourselves money bags which do not grow old, a treasure in the heavens that does not fail, where no thief approaches nor moth destroys.
>
> —Luke 12:33

When helping a Believer financially, it is important to find out what happened to their previous money. Were they good stewards or did they simply mismanage it? God generally asks us to give to others to help meet their needs, not their wants and desires.

> For I do not mean that others should be eased
> and you burdened;

—2 Corinthians 8:13

Provide for Your Own

The most basic level of giving must be within our own families. You must meet your family's needs. This is not limited to your children, but also includes your parents and grandparents. You must not forget that once you are married, you have two sets of parents—not one! God said to honor your father and mother, and that commandment is not just for young children!

God will not tolerate an attitude of indifference toward our parents. The responsibility of providing for family members who cannot provide for themselves rests with you, not the church or the government!

What do you do when grown children ask for help?

The answer is easy. You do exactly what you should do with other people. Evaluate the need and the reason for the need and then determine if you should help, as well as what type of help they really need.

God condemns dishonesty! Honesty is the best policy! False words are not only evil in themselves, but they infect the soul with evil. We must require complete honesty from our grown children when evaluating their need for help.

It is good to help your children face the reality of the decisions that they have made. If you have not done so previously, teach your children to work so that they will have money and to save so that they will have a surplus and give!

> But if anyone does not provide for his own, and
> especially for those of his household, he has de-
> nied the faith and is worse than an unbeliever.

—1 Timothy 5:8

> If any believing man or woman has widows, let
> them relieve them, and do not let the church be
> burdened, that it may relieve those who are re-
> ally widows.
>
> —1 Timothy 5:16

Sharing within the Body

It is unimaginable that there are hungry Christians, but there are!

God requires us to share with the Body of Christ—the church. According to 1 John 3:17-18, if we have a surplus, see a brother in need, and fail to help them, the love of God does not abide in us. You demonstrate love through your words and your actions. Help others according to your ability!

Christianity does not suffer from a lack of money. The Body, as a whole, has all the money that it needs. It is a matter of your commitment to God to obey His financial principles, which includes helping those within the Body who have needs.

> If a brother or sister is naked and destitute of
> daily food, and one of you says to them, "Depart
> in peace, be warmed and filled," but you do not
> give them the things which are needed for the
> body, what does it profit?
>
> —James 2:15-16

In March 1995, I wrote the following in a letter to family and friends. I believe that it will help you understand the significance of giving in the life of the Believer, and to see clearly that God loves a cheerful giver and that He will pour out blessing upon their life. Now when I say blessings, I am not speaking only, or primarily, of financial blessing. God frequently blesses the giver with something much better than money—a closer and deeper relationship with Him.

First, I wrote, "I feel so blessed to have a wife who willingly sacrifices in order to help meet the needs of others." Then later in the letter, I expounded on what Pam had done. "We have started a food pantry. We share the food with people who come and express a need. We give food to four or five people each week. Last week a lady came and asked for help. She said her sister sent her to us and told her, 'Those people are very kind and they will help you.' She cried when we gave her the food. We were able to meet some of her physical needs. It is our prayer that we will meet the spiritual needs of the people along with the physical needs."

Two months later, I wrote about the same topic.

"God has really been blessing in this area of our ministry. Last month someone called us from Texas and said that if we would drive to the border they would fill our van with food for our ministry. They not only filled our van but also gave us tracts, Bibles, Christian literature, and a six-month supply of blood pressure medicine. Then they told us, 'We will give you supplies once a month.' What a blessing!"

The best way to describe how much they gave us is to tell you what happened when I brought it home.

When we brought the food into our home, I stacked it on our table. Then we needed to leave the house. When we returned, just at the exact time I was putting the key in the door, I heard a loud crash. I thought we were being robbed again! I ran to the back of the house where I met my son Michael. No robbers were found. We started looking for the source of the noise and we found it in the dining room. The table had collapsed under the weight of all the food that I had stacked on top of it. The leaf broke, and two legs were sheared off. Needless to say, we are getting a new table.

The people who gave us the food are with Way of The Cross Ministries, a missionary support organization helping more than four hundred different missionaries with their work. They received our name from another mission group called Feed the Children. Our friend, Skip Purcell, had gone to visit the director of Feed the Children. While they were talking, Skip pulled out our letter and showed it to him. That director did not know us. He had never even met us. Yet the Spirit of the living God prompted him to help us. So he sent a fax to Way of The Cross Ministries, a sister organization, and encouraged them to help supply the food that we needed.

We must hold our possessions loosely. As soon as we feel the prompting of the Spirit of God, we must be willing and ready to release whatever we have and invest it in the lives of those around us. If you will do that, you, like Pam and me, will be blessed beyond measure—even more than your table can hold!

Do Not Muzzle the Ox

For some reason, many Christians think that the pastor should live at a lower standard than others. If you have friends in the ministry, you should help support them financially. Your missionary friends have gone out in the name of Jesus to help bring others into the Kingdom of God. They do not get their support from the unsaved, but from the saved. Send them out in a manner pleasing to God. It does not mean that you have to support them in a lavish lifestyle.

Many missionaries are in a worse situation than local pastors are. They are barely able to meet their current obligations and are unable to set aside anything for their long-term needs.

Christian schoolteachers are among the neediest in the church today. They are very committed people, but they can only live at that pay level for a time. Then they must exit and look for work that will meet the needs of their families.

These situations are a blight on Christianity. We need to find the solution for these situations. A solider in the King's army has to live. God commands those who hear the Word to support those who deliver it.

Support your pastor. Support the Christian schoolteachers that you know. Find a missionary who has an effective work for the Lord and support him "in a manner worthy of God."

Be Discerning

Unfortunately, ministries and other groups that are poorly managed, and sometimes dishonest, have inundated the church. When you give, you must be discerning about where your money goes.

You must be certain that the missionary or ministry that you are giving to is giving a message that is true to the Word of God. Are the leaders living in a godly manner? Are they growing? Is there a standard of excellence in all that they do? Do they waste resources?

> For it is written in the law of Moses, "You shall not muzzle an ox while it treads out the grain." Is it oxen God is concerned about? Or does He say it altogether for our sakes? For our sakes, no doubt, this is written, that he who plows should plow in hope, and he who threshes in hope should be

partaker of his hope. If we have sown spiritual things for you, is it a great thing if we reap your material things?

—1 Corinthians 9:9-11

Reach Out and Touch Someone!

Beloved, you do faithfully whatever you do for the brethren and for strangers, who have borne witness of your love before the church. If you send them forward on their journey in a manner worthy of God, you will do well.

—3 John 1:5-6

Even so the Lord has commanded that those who preach the gospel should live from the gospel.

—1 Corinthians 9:14

God also directs us to give to the unsaved people who live among us. One of the greatest witnesses that the church can have in the community is to help meet the physical needs of the unsaved. Care about people, and you will make an impact in the lives of many for the Kingdom of God.

And whoever gives one of these little ones only a cup of cold water in the name of a disciple, assuredly, I say to you, he shall by no means lose his reward.

—Matthew 10:42

He who gives to the poor will not lack, but he who hides his eyes will have many curses.

—Proverbs 28:27

Just before beginning the Church at Baratillo, a friend who lived in Mexico told me that the missionaries and pastors from the previous generation had made a significant error when they first came and saw the tremendous economic struggles of the people living in the outlying villages. He went on to say that, in helping to meet their physical needs, they had forgotten to teach them that it is more blessed to give than to receive.

What he was saying is, they were teaching the people how to receive but not teaching them how to give!

As Believers, we must learn the truth of the Scripture — it truly is more blessed to give than to receive. I am not saying, and I will never say, that if you give financially God will automatically give you back more financially. But if you give as the Lord leads, He will pour out spiritual blessing on your life that are far greater than anything that you could possibly receive in the financial realm.

Giving is not just about money. We must also share the most valuable thing that we have with those around us.

> Then Peter said, "Silver and gold I do not have,
> but what I do have I give you: In the name of Jesus
> Christ of Nazareth, rise up and walk."

> —Acts 3:6

One year, most of the farmers in our area had a very challenging situation. For the first time in many years, the rains started early. By late March and early April most were planting corn as well as tending to their trees. Hopes were high for a good season. Well, a few weeks later a frost killed part of the blossoms and left many people discouraged. A few more weeks passed and the rains stopped. Most of the corn remained small and produced only a few ears for feeding the chickens.

At harvest time, the buyers usually come to each farmer and make an agreement to purchase their apples. That year they did not come. The county government made an official estimation that over 300,000 bushels of apples were not purchased and either rotted on the tree or spoiled after harvest. Many of our neighbors found themselves in this situation.

Those who had children who owned a truck would take twenty-five or thirty bushels into town at a time and sell them in different parts of the city. The others just sat and waited, hoping someone would come and buy the apples. One day, when Nathan and I were talking, I thought aloud about helping Poncho with his apples.

How? Then I thought I could buy a vanload of apples and try to resell them in the city. When I asked Pam about the idea, she was in complete agreement.

The next day, after taking all the seats out of the van, Samuel and I went to Poncho's orchard and told him that we had a buyer for some apples. When he asked me, "Who?" I told him that I was the buyer. He looked strangely at me and said, "What are you going to do with that many apples?" I told him that I planned to take them into town and resell them—and if I made any profit it was all for him. Six hours later, we had the first eighty bushels loaded in the van. As Samuel and I pulled out of the orchard, Samuel asked me, "What are we going to do with all these apples?" I told him that we would sell them if it was God's will and then we would come back for more. With that, we bowed our heads and prayed a short prayer. "Lord, show yourself strong not only to Poncho, but also to Samuel and me, as well as to everyone else in this valley."

At 2:30 the next afternoon, Samuel and I pulled back into Poncho's orchard. He looked surprised to see me. Stepping out of the van, I handed him the profit I had made from selling the apples. Then I told him I was ready to take another load into town. Over the next few days, Poncho and two workers spent their time getting all his apples ready for the market. My children and I spent our days loading apples and taking them into town to sell. When I brought the profit from the last apples to Poncho, he was very grateful that he had made almost 50% more than he would have had the buyer come and bought his apples. This really helped him since his final crop was smaller than normal.

After I finished talking to Poncho, Samuel and I got back in the van to head home. I was tired and sore from moving the apples around and ready for a rest. While starting the van, I looked up and saw Tacho standing beside his apples. He had a buyer, so I pulled up and, in an effort to make conversation, I asked him when the buyer would be there. He told me that he had picked up part of them and did not know for sure if the buyer was coming back. I thought of 1 John 3:17: "But whoso hath this world's good, and seeth his brother have need, and shutteth up his bowels of compassion from him, how dwelleth the love of God in him?" I quickly said that I would be glad to take them into town and try to sell them. Much to my surprise, the next day he told me that he wanted to take me up on the offer to carry the apples into town.

When Tacho, Samuel and I were pulling into the market, I looked at Tacho and said, "I don't know where a buyer is but God does. Let's pray and ask Him to help us sell the apples." Tacho agreed and I prayed that God would help us find a buyer. Less than two hours later we were on our way home. Tacho had sold all his apples. In less than a week, the Lord allowed us to find buyers for almost 15,000 pounds of apples.

Divine Appointments

In the early part of 2000, I made a quick trip to Georgia for a truck. I took a bus there and then drove the truck back.

Nathan drove me to the bus station in McAllen. A few minutes after we arrived, my bus pulled in so I told Nathan he could go ahead and leave. I boarded the bus. After sitting there for almost an hour, they told us that the driver had gotten sick and they were looking for a replacement. Another hour passed and we still had no driver. I got off the bus to ask how much longer it would be when one of the workers said, "A bus is leaving right now to go to Houston." I quickly boarded. It pulled out of the station as soon as I took my seat.

A few minutes later, the bus stopped and picked up another passenger. Then another. Then another. By this time, I was a little worried so I asked the driver when we would be in Houston. He said, "We will be in Harlingen (a town about thirty miles from McAllen) in about two hours. Then you can get a bus to Houston from there!" I knew that I would miss my first connection and that would make me miss every other one. I wondered why this had happened.

As I was sitting there thinking about the extra time that I would be on the bus, I realized that I had not eaten in a long time, so I pulled out the bag of food that my daughter Misty had made for me. I asked the elderly lady that was sitting next to me if she had eaten. She had not, so we shared a meal. As it turned out, she had had a stroke several months before. Since getting out of the hospital, she had been living in a mini-storage room because she could not afford a hotel. She was going to Harlingen to find her bother.

We were able to spend some sweet time in Christian fellowship over lunch. When we parted company, I gave her enough food for the rest of the day and made sure she could get a hotel that night.

On the next leg of my journey, I began to talk to a Hispanic fellow that was sitting close by. He was telling me about the trouble that he was having with his teenage son. I just "happened" to have the latest issue of our magazine with me and it just "happened" to include an article titled "Winning the Heart of a Rebel". He immediately began reading it. An hour later, he looked up and said, "Thank you for giving this to me. This is exactly what I needed!"

When I arrived in Houston, a fellow who had been on my original bus was there too. We talked for a while. After I testified to him, he told me that he had already trusted Christ but that he was still battling several sins in his life. I was able to share with him about being an overcomer in Christ. He was encouraged.

When I got on my next bus there was only one seat open—next to a wild-looking fellow in his early twenties. He just sat there with his arms crossed. I was praying about how to share the gospel with him. Once again, I got my bag out and asked if he would like to share a meal with me.

Immediately, his whole countenance changed. The food had given me the open door that I was looking for. We talked through most of the night. He had left California to go and visit his mom in Florida. She was dying of cancer. He only had enough money to take the bus. He had not eaten since he left California. I spent several hours explaining the gospel to him. God planted seeds in his life that day. Seeds that, I believe, will grow into a new life in Christ.

My last layover was to be about five hours, and then a short ninety-minute bus ride to my mother's. She had decided to pick me up at that stop so I would not have to wait the extra time. As we were riding to her house, I no longer wondered why I was delayed. I had several divine appointments that God had arranged. The situations that seem so disturbing when they happen are God's way of helping us to keep our minds and hearts focused on Him.

A Changed Man

Close to the end of our 2011 conference in Guadalajara, three women approached my wife and asked if I would be willing to meet with their nephew. He was a young cartel member who was wounded in a shootout between two rival gangs. After thinking about the situation, I agreed to meet with him on the condition that he attend the final conference session. My scheduled topic was about preparing your children for their eternal destination. He came to the meeting and listened attentively. Following the session, he and I sat down and talked for a long time. He was 25 years old. One of the gangs kidnapped his mother, father, and brother seven months ago. Less than two weeks before, he was involved in a shootout between gangs. After he was shot, his buddies helped him to a car and he escaped.

He expressed a deep desire to return and "make" them tell him what happened to his parents.

Later, when I asked him if he was ready to become a follower of Jesus, he told me he knew that he should, but he wanted to go "get them" first. I looked him straight in the eye and said, "You know that if you go back they will likely kill you. Nevertheless, if you do get them first, their buddies will hunt you down and kill you. You will die one way or the other!"

I finally decided that it was time to end the conversation. I told him that I knew he came to meet me because he was searching for something. Then I added that he knew what he needed to do, but that he was not man enough to do it! He knew he needed to humble himself and ask God for forgiveness.

I think it shocked him when I told him that he was afraid because repentance might bring tears to his eyes and he was afraid to cry because he thought he was too tough. After that, I asked him, "Do you want to walk out the door the same way you came in, or do you want to walk out as a new man—a changed man—in Christ?" He slowly tilted his head and indicated he wanted to get right with God. He prayed a heart-felt prayer of repentance, clearly confessing his sins and then asking God to lead him, give him wisdom, and guide his life. He also asked that God would use him. He stood up a different man—a changed man.

On a different occasion, I spoke at length with a soldier, Sergeant Medina, for well over an hour. He was the platoon leader who was in charge of all the men at this roadblock. He not only shared his fears and concerns with me; he also shared the hopes and dreams that he had for his children. He asked me for literature for the thirty men in his platoon.

There is a war that is raging within the borders of Mexico—a war for the hearts, lives, and souls of men. This is a spiritual battle. Satan is not holding anything back in this battle. He is fighting to win. We must give it our all. We must fight the good fight. We must be found faithful in our service for the King of kings and the Lord of lords.

Giving to Build Faith in God

We have considered giving to our families by meeting their needs, giving to help the family of God, and giving to help the unsaved. I would like to close this section by discussing giving to build faith in God. This type of giving is like a coin; it has two sides.

When you give, you are not only blessed more than the person who receives the gift, your faith is also strengthened. When you feel the prompting of the Spirit and obey, it makes it easier to obey the second time. With each additional gift you give, God stretches and strengthens you. You are learning to think about others and their needs and not just what you need or want. I encourage you to step out in faith and begin giving.

The other side of this coin is building the faith of the receiver. When a person prays for a specific need and God uses you to meet that need, the receiver's faith increases. Many times, the Lord will use your gift like a springboard to catapult the receiver into a deeper relationship with Himself.

Sometimes you may not understand the significance of your gifts for decades or until eternity. Nevertheless, rest assured, God is using every one of them for His purposes.

The next two stories are examples from my life, in which God used a gift to increase our faith in Him.

Red Jell-O

In early 1981, I was sitting at the table with my family when I noticed that Pam was dishing up Jell-O—red Jell-O—for breakfast. When I questioningly glanced at her, she quietly whispered, "This is all the food that we have left in the house!" The prayer that followed and its answer provided the foundation for building a life that is fully and completely dependent on God. This is not the story of a man of great faith; it is the story of how a great God blesses a little faith.

This happened just after I received Christ as my Savior. I was married. I had three children. I was going to college. Moreover, I was working full time as a painting contractor during the day and I went to school at night. I worked hard, but I made little money. We were surviving, getting by. For a time, work was nonexistent. I was looking for work everyday, everywhere, trying to find a house to paint.

One morning I got up, walked into the dining room, and sat down. The three little kids were all excited. It was then that I noticed that Pam was dishing up Jell-O—red Jell-O—for breakfast.

I had not been a Christian very long. I had not shared a need for food with anyone.

We sat at the table and I prayed. I do not remember what I prayed, but surely, it was something like, "Thank You for the red Jell-O. Please provide something else."

With that, we ate our red Jell-O. The kids were happy and Daddy was worried.

I had already printed a thousand flyers advertising my painting services. I could usually count on getting five or six calls from that many flyers. As soon as breakfast was over, I went out and began passing them out. I went to the paint stores looking for work. I went to all of the contractors I knew.

By midafternoon, nothing had happened and this new Christian was discouraged because God did not meet all of my needs. If you are eating red Jell-O, you need more food. It was a need. I am not saying that sharing a need with others is wrong, but at that point in my life asking others for help was not what God wanted me to do.

I returned home and pulled my old beat-up paint truck into the driveway. I walked toward the house, shuffling my feet with my head down. I noticed a car in the driveway that belonged to Betty Owen, Pam's friend.

I opened the door and noticed that the house was messy. There were paper bags scattered all over the floor. My wife was standing on a chair, happily putting cans of food in the cabinet.

I looked at her, asking with my eyes, "What is going on? What is happening?"

Betty had been praying that morning, and God put us on her heart. She did not know anything about our need, but she went to the store and filled her trunk up with meats, vegetables, canned goods—everything that you would need to stock a kitchen. Now this was back when cars were big and trunks were even bigger. She had filled up her entire trunk with food and brought it to our family, not because we shared that need with her, but because God had impressed our need on her heart and she decided to meet it.

Many times God will impress things on your heart. It is important to follow His leading.

Years later this story, and a few others like it, helped my family and me to go on the mission field—fifteen days after we made the decision to go.

God Has a Sense of Humor

Few people ever think of a bar of soap as a significant need. Fewer still ever pray specifically for one. That is, unless you do not have any soap and you do have three dirty little children. Then your husband calls to tell you that he will be home shortly and that the kids need to be clean and ready to go.

A few months after I received Christ, we realized that my grandmother was in the advanced stages of Alzheimer's disease. She was very sick. My grandfather was taking care of her. Everyone thought she was going to die soon.

I was going to visit her on my lunch hour three times a week. I would read the Bible with her and talk to her.

My grandfather worked at a Christian campground. He worked hard. He would get up early and work several hours before my grandmother woke up, then he would go home and fix breakfast for the two of them. One day he came in, sat down in his chair, and died. It was a real surprise. No warning, no prior notice—nothing. He just died. It was hard.

All of my aunts and uncles, along with my mother and father, got together to figure out what to do. They decided that my grandmother would go live with her oldest daughter. They immediately began cleaning out the house since that daughter lived in another state. In addition, the house was on the campground so it needed to be vacated for the next caretaker. My mother found, in the back closet, a couple of huge bags full of things. Do you remember when they used brown paper grocery bags? They were massive. My mother just wanted to get rid of the things.

My mother said to her siblings, "Mike is here. Let's give them to him. He lives close by." I looked in the bags and thought, "I do not want this stuff!" Nevertheless, it was my mother so I said, "Sure, I will be happy to take the bags home." I put them in the car and then called my wife to tell her to get the kids cleaned up. I added, "I'll be home in a little while and we will all go to the funeral home for the viewing and to visit the family."

When I got home, I took the sacks in and gave them to Pam. I was expecting the same kind of reaction that I had had when I looked into the bags. Instead, she looked in the bags and exclaimed with excitement, "Wow."

At that point in our life, we did not have very much money, and Pam did not have any money. When I called, the kids had been out playing all day. We all know what happens when little kids play outside all day. They were dirty and Pam did not have any soap in the house.

For many years (I do not know how long, but due to the quantity of soap in my grandmother's bags, it had to be ten or fifteen years), my grandparents had been collecting bars of soap! Earlier when I had called, Pam had prayed, "Lord, will you send me a bar of soap?"

Now the Lord has a sense of humor. He sent two huge bags of soap! Seven years that soap lasted. Seven years! My grandfather had saved soap so that we would have enough soap for our growing family to last for seven years. For seven years, we did not buy a bar of soap. It ran out just before we came to Mexico.

When we arrived in Mexico, some of the people from the church that had invited us had a housewarming party. Many of those ladies brought us soap. We had many different sizes and colors of soap. Even today, people will come from the United States to visit us and bring things that we might not be able to get here in Mexico. Many of them bring us soap!

This story not only shows that God is interested in every need that we have, it also demonstrates that God has a sense of humor. He answers our prayers and meets our every need, no matter what it is.

I Owe a Debt of Gratitude

These two stories are like thousands of other stories where God met a specific need at a specific time and no one other than God could have done it. I have repeated these stories many times since they happened. By doing so, I am increasing my faith and the faith of others.

It is important that, when you hear the prompting of the Holy Spirit, you obey, because you do not know what He is going to do. A big God blesses just a little faith. It is through our faith in Him that we can accomplish anything of lasting value.

God used these stories to build my faith in Him and to prepare me for what He was calling me to do. I had the faith to step out of my comfort zone and come to Mexico fifteen days after making the decision to come because of what the Lord taught me through these two stories. I owe a debt of gratitude to Betty Owen and my mother. God transformed my life using these events to begin that process of building my faith. Then again, I am not the only one who owes them that debt. So does every person who has been touched by the hand of God since we came to Mexico. In the same way, so do you!

Do not take this section lightly. By learning to be a cheerful giver, you can literally touch the life of someone for an eternity. Perhaps, just perhaps, God will give you a little glimpse this side of eternity of your impact.

Chapter 14

Applying God's Wisdom

The LORD by wisdom founded the earth; by understanding He established the heavens.

—Proverbs 3:19

It helps to have a list of principles when making decisions about applying God's wisdom. These are not like the law of the Medes and the Persians that can never be changed. They are simply financial guidelines that God has given to make us more effective for the Kingdom of God.

If we trust God and seek Him with our whole hearts, we will find His wisdom and His direction for our lives. We are not to lean upon anything other than God and His Word.

When God takes the message of Jesus Christ and mixes it with simple messengers, all the glory goes to God. God does not need your intelligence nor mine. God does not need our money. God does not need our personalities. God also does not need our abilities or our fame. These are not the things that God seeks in us!

Do you know what God seeks? God is seeking your availability! God is not seeking your education; he is seeking a relationship with you! He is looking for simple people who are filled with the Holy Spirit—people who are fully committed to Him!

What is the main quality or characteristic that God is seeking in the lives of those He will use? It is humility! The humility that recognizes it is God who changes lives! People who can say, "God, I am nothing. You are everything!"

Acknowledge God's ownership—accept the fact that you are a steward. Learn to praise God when things are going well, as well as during the lean times. You must truly get to the point where you understand that God owns it all.

It is one thing to put on a facade of Christianity; it is another thing to be completely dedicated to an all-powerful God and to allow Him to do His work in your life so that you will become useful to God and used by the Creator of the universe—to do His will here on this earth.

> **And so find favor and high esteem in the sight of God and man. Trust in the LORD with all your heart, and lean not on your own understanding; in all your ways acknowledge Him, And He shall direct your paths.**
>
> **—Proverbs 3:4-6**

Surrender, commit, and obey—these are not only the prerequisites to becoming a follower of Christ, but also to becoming financially free in Christ.

Surrender your finances to God. Let Him lead and guide you completely in this area of life. Commit everything in your life to Him, including your finances. Obey God in all areas of life—especially finances.

> **Then He said to them all, "If anyone desires to come after Me, let him deny himself, and take up his cross daily, and follow Me."**
>
> **—Luke 9:23**

Accept God's direction. Do not just assume that you know His will. Seek Him and understand His will before moving forward. "Seek ye first the Kingdom of God ..."

Never make investments that will put your financial security at risk. There is nothing wrong with investing, but avoid speculation. Do not buy things you do not understand. Do not borrow to invest.

> **For which of you, intending to build a tower, does not sit down first and count the cost, whether he has enough to finish it.**
>
> **—Luke 14:28**

Keep your bills current and your bank account balanced.

Do not buy anything on credit that you cannot pay for in full when the bill is due. When you can pay so easily with a credit card, is using cash realistic? Yes, because paying with cash will benefit you the most.

> **And having food and clothing, with these we shall be content.**
>
> **—1 Timothy 6:8**

It has been proven that you will, on average, spend less with cash. Using a debit or credit card can be more convenient, but that does not mean that it is really your best option. A study found that people spend 12–18% more when they use credit cards instead of cash[3]. Think about that for a moment—let it sink in.

You are more likely to stick to your budget when you pay with cash. Letting go of cash is very emotional. It is much harder to make impulse purchases when paying cash.

You will not go into debt when paying cash. Using a credit card is a slippery slope. You will not owe anyone if you pay with cash because you are spending what is already yours!

Learn to distinguish between your basic needs and your wants and desires.

> **While, through the proof of this ministry, they glorify God for the obedience of your confession**

---

[3] The Money Answer Book, Dave Ramsey

to the gospel of Christ, and for your liberal sharing with them and all men.

—2 Corinthians 9:13

Do not go into debt to do God's work. If God wants it done, He
can pay for it. Debt will divert you from God's plan and His
purpose for your life. Credit is a way to avoid trusting in God. Do
not tempt the Lord with debt. Seek Him and ask Him to provide
ahead of time.

Give, rather than lend, to the needs of others. The result of
loaning to other Believers is frequently a loss of friendship and
fellowship. Giving will be a testimony to your commitment to them
and to the Lord.

Avoid cosigning for anyone—even your children. When you
cosign, you are helping a person do what God never intended for
them to do. Cosigning is your pledge to pay the debts of another,
and Scripture forbids this as surety.

My son, if you become surety for your friend, if
you have shaken hands in pledge for a stranger,
You are snared by the words of your mouth; You
are taken by the words of your mouth.

—Proverbs 6:1-2

A man devoid of understanding shakes hands in a
pledge, and becomes surety for his friend.

—Proverbs 17:18

Take the garment of one who is surety for a stranger,
and hold it as a pledge when it is for a seductress.

—Proverbs 20:16

Take the garment of him who is surety for a
stranger, and hold it in pledge when he is surety
for a seductress.

—Proverbs 27:13

> A man of great wrath will suffer punishment; for if
> you rescue him, you will have to do it again.

> —Proverbs 19:19

Evaluate every purchase you make. Make wise decisions. Never make financial decision when you are in a hurry. Learn patience.

> But also for this very reason, giving all diligence,
> add to your faith virtue, to virtue knowledge, to
> knowledge self-control, to self-control persever-
> ance, to perseverance godliness.

> —2 Peter 1:5-6

Make the sacrifices that are necessary and do not overextend yourself. Do not overwork. Learn the proper balance between work, home, family, and church.

> Do not overwork to be rich; Because of your own
> understanding, cease! Will you set your eyes on
> that which is not? For riches certainly make them-
> selves wings; they fly away like an eagle toward
> heaven.

> —Proverbs 23:4-5

Remember that God sees the end from the beginning. Accept what He sends along and learn what He wants to teach you.

> I know how to be abased, and I know how to
> abound. Everywhere and in all things I have
> learned both to be full and to be hungry, both to
> abound and to suffer need. I can do all things
> through Christ who strengthens me.

> —Philippians 4:12-13

If you do not have peace about it, do not do it. Being overly involved emotionally with a financial decision tends to cause you to overlook God's principles and to begin leaning on your own understanding.

Rest in the LORD, and wait patiently for Him.

—Psalms 37:7

Accept God's direction. He may be taking you through a trial to teach you something. Accept these situations and learn from them. When you have a financial need or a project to complete, pray. Learn that God knows your needs even before you do and that He is faithful in supplying them. It is often through the giving or withholding of finances that He gives you final direction.

The blessing of the LORD makes one rich, And He adds no sorrow with it.

—Proverbs 10:22

Give with an open heart and He will bless you abundantly. First, you must surrender your plans to God and live within the plans that He has for you. Sometimes what we use for the Lord has a price. Sometimes we have to make personal sacrifices to serve Him. However, such sacrifices are always worth making. The benefits are always much greater than the sacrifices.

I am not saying, and I will never say, that we are to expect that God will give us more material blessing if we make more material sacrifices. When we make material sacrifices God gives us something of greater value—an intimate relationship with Him. God confirms this concept in Luke 12:34: "For where your treasure is, there your heart will be also." Whatever it may cost, the deepest desire of your heart should be to be the person that God uses.

Chapter 15

How to Have a Successful Marriage

Communication is of utmost importance in any relationship, but especially marriage. When a couple begins to talk about their finances and plan their family's budget together, finances typically become their best area of communication. The marriage is strengthened and built up.

This book is not about marriage, but if you learn to communicate effectively in the area of finances, it will become the springboard for a successful marriage. It is for that reason it is appropriate to take a few moments to discuss marriage.

In successful marriages:

- Spouses give up their rights.
- Wives give respect to their husbands.
- Husbands love their wives.
- Both give Christ their reverence.
- Spouses do not hold back their love for each other.

204 For the Love of ~~Money~~ God

- Both spouses learn to put aside bitterness. (Now that is true forgiveness!)
- Both husband and wife work regularly to rekindle their feelings for each other.
- Both spouses find and experience the love of God in their lives.

Men and women are different physically, emotionally and relationally. We process things differently. We often think differently. We can experience the same situation, at the same time, and see it from a very different perspective.

In a successful marriage, both the husband and wife experience joy and unity, even amid financial struggles. A successful marriage comes from uniting physically, emotionally and spiritually. This concept goes back to how God created man and woman. He created us to be united.

> And Adam said: "This is now bone of my bones
> And flesh of my flesh; She shall be called Woman,
> Because she was taken out of Man." Therefore a
> man shall leave his father and mother and be
> joined to his wife, and they shall become one
> flesh.
>
> —Genesis 2:23-24

God ordained marriage. Husband and Wife, unite your hearts and minds. It is at that point that you will experience the joy of marriage as God intended. Many times, you do not have this type of joy in your marriage relationship because you are self-centered, especially in finances. The husband does not hesitate to buy a new tool that he will use once a year, but if the wife buys a new appliance that she will use every day, it creates a financial crisis in his mind.

You say you believe God and His word, but do you really believe Him with your finances—in your marriage?

> By this all will know that you are My disciples, if
> you have love for one another.
>
> —John 13:35

God's Word is true. Trust Him and follow His guidelines for your finances and your marriage. In successful marriages, spouses give up their rights for one another.

Submitting to one another in the fear of God.

—Ephesians 5:21

Submitting means to place oneself under another.

In a successful marriage—in successful relationships of any kind—we give up our rights. Today people tend to relate submission with weakness and joylessness. Some think that if they give up their rights, they will be walked over and will never experience joy, or that they need to protect their rights to experience joy.

Yes, to give up your rights for someone else is risky, but Christ often calls us to do the opposite of what the world thinks is right. Lose your life and you will find it. The first will be last and the last will be first. Do not repay evil with evil, but with blessings.

Giving up your rights, submitting to each other, is what the Lord calls you to do. It is the best and safest thing to do. Giving up your rights to your spouse is not about being weak. It requires great strength to give up your rights willingly.

Wives, submit to your own husbands, as to the Lord. For the husband is head of the wife, as also Christ is head of the church; and He is the Savior of the body. Therefore, just as the church is subject to Christ, so let the wives be to their own husbands in everything. Husbands, love your wives, just as Christ also loved the church and gave Himself for her, that He might sanctify and cleanse her with the washing of water by the word, that He might present her to Himself a glorious church, not having spot or wrinkle or any such thing, but that she should be holy and without blemish. So husbands ought to love their own wives as their own bodies; he who loves his wife loves himself. For no one ever hated his own flesh, but nourishes and cherishes it, just as the Lord does the church. For we are members of His

> body, of His flesh and of His bones. *For this rea-*
> *son a man shall leave his father and mother and be*
> *joined to his wife, and the two shall become one*
> *flesh.* This is a great mystery, but I speak con-
> cerning Christ and the church. Nevertheless let
> each one of you in particular so love his own wife
> as himself, and let the wife see that she respects
> her husband.

> —Ephesians 5:17-33

Jesus is our example. He was not weak, yet He willingly gave up what was His—for us. Jesus, God in the flesh, submitted Himself to become human. He submitted Himself to the authorities. He submitted Himself to the cross.

No one forced Him to do any of these things, but He did so willingly because of His desire to glorify the Father and because of His love for you. That takes strength! That is love! That is what God is calling you to do for your spouse!

> Wives, submit to your own husbands, as is fitting
> in the Lord. Husbands, love your wives and do
> not be bitter toward them.

> —Colossians 3:18-19

Be strong and be willing to give up your rights for one another so you can glorify the Father and begin to experience the joy that submission will bring into your life.

Paul gets more specific concerning some of the differences in the way that God has designed us.

He tells wives that in successful marriages the wife gives respect to her husband. If you truly want to experience a successful marriage, you need to respect your husband.

God, in His wisdom, has given men the need to feel respected. Perhaps this is why He tells wives to respect their husbands; it fulfills a God-designed need. When a wife gives respect to her husband, she is demonstrating love to him.

Some might think, *My husband does not deserve my respect.* It is not about your husband deserving respect. It is about you trusting God. By respecting your husband, you honor and love your husband.

How do you show respect to someone whom you feel is not worthy of respect?

It begins with trusting God; that trust will overflow to your actions. If we really believe God is God and that His ways are best, then we will be able to do what He says.

What can you do to show respect?

- Pray for your husband daily.
- Remember that God will lead through your husband.
- Make a list of your husband's good qualities and review them regularly.
- Tell your husband what you appreciate about him.
- Do not criticize your husband to others, especially to your children.
- Look for the positive side of things that you may find irritating.
- Respond to his loving advances with enthusiasm.

If you are concerned about a decision your husband has made, talk to him sincerely in the following: "I am confused about such and such. Can you explain it to me? Can we talk about this?"

If you find yourself thinking negative thoughts about your husband, stop and choose to think of his good qualities.

Casting down arguments and every high thing that exalts itself against the knowledge of God, bringing every thought into captivity to the obedience of Christ

—2 Corinthians 10:5

Remember, God is working on you and your husband. Give God the freedom to teach your husband through failure. In the same way, give God the freedom to teach you to trust Him through your husband's failure.

Respect your husband in your actions.

In successful marriages, husbands give love to their wives.

Husbands, you need to love your wife as Christ loved the church. Christ loved the church sacrificially. We need to love our wives sacrificially. Now some may think, I sacrifice for my wife and family. I work long hours to provide. I would lay down my life to protect them from harm. We need to understand what sacrifice is.

Loving our wives sacrificially is going to look more like this: spending time talking about your day and her day, really listening to her, listening to the things going on in her life. Study your wife and act upon the things you learn. What does she like? Learn the little things and do them, the way she likes them done.

Discover her love language:

- Acts of Service
- Words of Affirmation
- Physical Touch
- Receiving Gifts
- Quality Time

You cannot just get married and tell her you love her, and then think that should be good enough for the rest of your days.

God has designed your wife with a need to feel love from you. God has given you responsibilities to meet that need in your wife by showing her love in the way she will receive it. It will require sacrifice on your part. Opening up about finances is one of the best ways to demonstrate love to your wife.

Now just so we understand, both husbands and wives need to love and respect. Love and respect are like food and water for the heart. You need both to survive, but you can live longer without food than water. Men and women have different water.

For men, respect is like water, while love is like food. For women, love is like water and respect like food. Therefore, husbands, you need to love your wives sacrificially. Wives, you need to respect your husbands. We are to submit to one another out of the fear of the Lord.

To experience success in finances, to experience the most successful marriage possible, to experience the best life possible requires a personal relationship with Christ. Being in a relationship with Christ is the only way to experience the fullness of life that Christ has come to offer us.

When we receive Christ as Savior and have the presence of the Holy Spirit in our lives, God enables us to love, sacrifice, respect, and submit ourselves beyond our own strength, because now we can operate and act in the strength of the Holy Spirit.

Simply put, the stability of marriage is a by-product of an iron-willed determination to make it work, and this requires a constant conscious effort to stop demanding your own rights, and to show love and respect for each other.

> **But I want you to know that the head of every man is Christ, the head of woman is man, and the head of Christ is God.**
>
> **—1 Corinthians 11:3**

Communication is vital to your financial planning as a family. For that reason, I encourage you to answer the following questions and then discuss them with your spouse.

Be very careful to use these questions to improve your communication, not to attack your spouse. Answer these questions truthfully, as if your spouse was the person asking them to you.

- What are your top three goals in life?
- What are your goals for this year?
- How can I help you achieve your goals?
- What can you do to improve our financial situation?
- What can I do?
- Do you think that I maintain a proper balance between work, church and family?
- Do you think that you do?
- Are there things around the house that I need to take care of?
- What do you think should be my priorities outside the home?
- Do I need to make changes in my life?
- My attitudes?

A successful marriage is not just about staying together. It is about growing into the likeness and image of Christ together. With that thought in mind, let us continue with a few more questions.

- Are we closer in our marriage now compared to when we first got married?
- Do you feel that you are able to communicate with me in a way that I understand?
- Do you think that I communicate with you effectively?
- Am I sensitive to your needs?

- Am I patient with you?
- Do I criticize?
- Am I timely?
- Do I take you places often enough?
- Do I criticize you in front of others?
- Do I listen and truly consider your comments and suggestions?
- Do I talk to you enough?
- What was the last "little thing" I did for you that really encouraged you?
- What do I do that makes you angry?
- Do I demonstrate love to you?

Once you are married, it is likely that God has or will bless you with children. If you have children, ask the following questions as well.

- What are your goals as a family?
- Are we achieving them?
- What kind of family devotions should we have?
- Do we pray together?
- Do our children obey?
- Are we involved in the church in a way that pleases the Lord?
- Are we meeting the needs of the family?
- Do we make good use of our time?
- Do we watch too much TV?
- Are we training our children?

Most of the problems in the home revolve around finances and lack of communication. Ask these questions about how you are doing in this area:

- Do I handle money properly?
- Do you?
- What can we do to manage our finances better?
- Am I cheap?
- Am I extravagant?
- Do I accept my responsibility for the finances?
- Do we communicate about finances well?
- What are our financial goals?
- Is tithing necessary?

- How about giving?
- Do you like where we live and how we eat?

If you have made mistakes in handling your finances or your marriage, do not be discouraged by the consequences. Repent and then learn from them. Give thanks to God for them. For, you see, they are a result of His love for you.

> **My son, do not despise the chastening of the LORD, nor detest His correction; for whom the LORD loves He corrects, just as a father the son in whom he delights.**
>
> **—Proverbs 3:11-12**

Why is it that we, as adults, forget much about our childhood— our early years? Nevertheless, a few events are forged in our minds as long-lasting memories. My collection of random, long-lasting memories has had a significant impact in my life.

My earliest recollection is about something that happened when I was just three years old. Our family had made a trip to Tennessee to visit my grandparents. On the way home, we stopped at a lake to take a swim. After my dad dove off the edge, he floated to the surface but did not move. My mom finally realized that something was wrong and went to him. He had hit his head on a boulder that was just below the surface and fractured his neck. After my mom got him over the rock embankment to the shore, an ambulance came. I not only vividly remember the long drive to the hospital but also the terrified look on my mom's face. While the time frame escapes me, my father spent many months in the hospital—first in intensive care, then in traction, and finally in physical therapy.

My next memory begins when my dad returned home. He had a cast from his neck to his waist. At four, I became his constant companion and helper. He would sweep the floor but he could not bend over in his cast, so I would hold the dust pan for him.

Later, a neck brace replaced his cast. It was during this time that we made a trip into town. We bought a loaf of bread and stopped by a lake to feed the ducks. It was such great fun to see them running toward me and fighting over the bread that I tossed to them.

One day, decades later, my two-year-old granddaughter, Gracie, joined me on the ride to take people home from church. Gracie sat on my lap as we drove over the dirt roads to each of the houses. She talked and chattered the entire hour. We sang songs and talked about the surroundings. Being legally blind, Gracie could not see the lovely view, but I was able to describe it to her in vivid detail. I do not know if this will become one of her long-lasting memories, but I am certain it will be one of mine!

I began to think about my earliest memories. Why did I remember them? How can I help my kids and grandkids develop a set of good, life-changing memories during their early years?

My first memory was of a tragic accident. I remember it because of the fear of the unknown and the concern for the future. My next memory was of helping my dad sweep the floor. The more I think about it, the more I realize that I remember it because I felt needed—useful. I had a purpose in life: to help my dad.

The third memory was of feeding the ducks. I remembered that because it showed me how much my dad loved me. He wanted to show me appreciation for helping him do his daily tasks.

I think these memories show how we can help our children and grandchildren develop a set of good, life-changing memories during their early years. We need to show them, demonstrate to them, how they are needed and loved. Show them how God has a special plan for their lives.

It is a poor sort of memory that only works backwards!

Let us look forward and begin to develop memories for our children, our grandchildren and ourselves!

Perhaps we should put aside some of our business and go for a ride. "Look, Gracie, a rabbit is running across the road. It is hopping up and down as it runs. The car scares it, just like you get scared at buzzing noises. It is running wildly, trying to get out of the way, first to the right and then to the left. Its little, turned-up, white tail bounces up and down. If you could touch it, its grey fur and white tail would be soft."

We need to teach and train our children about finances, but more importantly, we need to show them the love of Christ through our actions. Be diligent with your finances but do not forget about taking time to be with your children!

I Slammed on the Brakes!

Early one morning we left home to pick up some supplies in Texas. It was in the cool of the morning as we drove down a winding, two-lane road.

Pam and I were having a delightful conversation when we rounded a curve. Without any notice or warning, there he was—in the middle of the road. I started to go left, but a tractor-trailer was in the other lane. To my right was a steep drop off—too steep to risk going over. I slammed on the brakes, but I could not stop! It was unavoidable! We hit him! An awful thud followed. Even before I stopped, I could smell the stench of death.

I did not know what to do. The accident followed us for many days.

Over the next several days, when we stopped our car people would ask what happened. Some would even turn their backs on us.

Every time I got into the van, I was strongly reminded of that day. It seemed like it would always be with me. I did not know how to get rid of it. I did not know if I could ever get rid of—of the smell of that skunk!

In much the same way, you may feel like you can never get out from under the financial burdens that you find yourself in today. Commit your ways to the Lord and He will direct your path. Then little by little, you will find yourself becoming free of the bondage.

Chapter 16

What Do I Do Now?

Information without practical application will be of no use to you or your family. This chapter will help you draw conclusions about the material that you have studied. Then you will be able to take those conclusions and apply them in your life. Take time to consider each area before moving on to the next topic.

1. Pray.

First, you must commit your life, your marriage and your finances to the Lord.

> Commit your works to the LORD, and your
> thoughts will be established.
>
> —Proverbs 16:3

2. Learn to become a steward instead of the owner of what God has entrusted to you.

> He who is faithful in what is least is faithful also in much; and he who is unjust in what is least is unjust also in much.
>
> —Luke 16:10

3. Give at least a tithe of all your income.

> Honor the LORD with your possessions, And with the firstfruits of all your increase.
>
> —Proverbs 3:9

4. Develop a budget.

A financial plan will help you to give an account of your finances to yourself and to God.

> Be diligent to know the state of your flocks, and attend to your herds; for riches are not forever, nor does a crown endure to all generations.
>
> —Proverbs 27:23-24

5. Pay off all credit cards and small loans.

> The rich rules over the poor, And the borrower is servant to the lender.
>
> —Proverbs 22:7

Pay off all debt. Living debt free liberates you for greater service in the Kingdom of God.

> The blessing of the LORD makes one rich, And He adds no sorrow with it.
>
> —Proverbs 10:22

6. Begin the process of teaching your children to be faithful stewards.

My son, hear the instruction of your father, and do
not forsake the law of your mother.

—Proverbs 1:8

Study well, apply these principles in your life, and then begin to
teach others what you have learned.

And the things that you have heard from me
among many witnesses, commit these to faithful
men who will be able to teach others also.

—2 Timothy 2:2

Chapter 17

He Will Raise Me Up

At fifty-two years old, I was crippled with Spondylitis and required surgery on my neck. During that time, I preached sitting down in a wheelchair, my body racked with pain. I knew beyond a doubt that God had called me to continue preaching the saving message of the Gospel of Jesus Christ.

Frequently, it is in times of trouble that people go into debt. It does not have to be that way. In order to not fall into that trap, we must make our decisions ahead of time—before financial problems arise.

First, let me go back to a letter that I began writing in 2011, but did not finish until the end of 2012. It was a difficult and challenging time in our lives.

Did the Richardsons Leave Mexico?

No, absolutely not! In spite of trials, difficulties, struggles, and even dangers, Pam and I firmly believe that God has called us to live our lives out in this, our beloved country. While some of the tools that we are using have changed, we continue to fight for the hearts, souls, and lives of our family as well as those around us.

When you read this letter, my prayer is that you will not only see my words but that you will also be able to hear my heart.

During the last year and a half, it has seemed like I was walking a tightrope—trying my best to do what is right in the face of ever-increasing and difficult circumstances. I have been keenly aware that a false move or a wrong decision could have devastating spiritual impacts for many years to come. While some of these circumstances are now behind us, it seems as if each week brings new trials and struggles, as well as opportunities for growth. Since I obviously cannot cover every event in detail, the following is a conglomeration of stories and events of the last eighteen months. During this time, we presented seven conferences, have done much evangelism work in dangerous areas, continued to pastor the church, and have also tried to stand firm against the vilest evil that Satan and his demons could bring.

While I was driving near Ciudad Mier, three men forced me off the road and out of my truck.

I had made a conscious decision to be in a dangerous area. Now what do I do with only a few seconds to decide—stay and submit or cut and run? Will I live or die? Will the church stand in the gap for my wife and kids?

I stopped and exited the truck. They interrogated me. Why was I there? What was I carrying? They inspected my vehicle. I was not scared—perhaps anxious or apprehensive.

They released me. I could leave.

When they turned toward their car, I called out, "You have talked to me, now I want to talk to you." They turned and I began sharing the Gospel. The leader asked if I was a Christian, then he added, "My wife is a Christian."

The Spirit fell upon me and I began to explain boldly that God had sent me to talk to him because of his wife's prayers.

When they were leaving, I told them that I had written a booklet especially for people like him but that I had just given out the last copy. I added, "Please stop me again so that I can give you a copy."

They left. Seeds had been planted.

We must never forget that God has called us to be faithful in sharing what we have with others. Remember that your salvation is the most valuable possession that you have. Share it freely with those whom God brings into your path.

In 2011, we had conferences in Obregon, Fronteras and Saltillo, as well as a series of four conferences in May of that year. Kevin Swanson came from Colorado to preach at the Saltillo conference and then he went to Mier to do some radio programs. We are grateful for his sacrifices and availability.

In May, our car was burglarized. It happened the morning that we were leaving Guadalajara to go to Cuernavaca. We had just finished the Pachuca and Guadalajara conferences, as well as five special services in churches and one in a Bible institute. At the time, there were three vehicles and a trailer in our caravan. We had stopped for breakfast. The only vehicle to be broken into was the one that I was using.

In the burglary, I lost my primary computer and a lot of software. We also lost all the titles and paperwork for three vehicles and the trailer, all my personal banking information, and other personal papers. I had about $2500 of emergency cash in my backpack. While we could now debate the wisdom of carrying enough cash to cover a major car breakdown, I had done that for the last 18 years.

I was carrying the cash from the book sales as well. A carrying case containing our portable recording equipment was stolen. The total loss was close to $17,000, including the cash.

Some have called me a fool; others say I am a Gringo loco—Crazy American—for going where I go, for doing the things that I do—especially when I travel into the violent areas of the country. Perhaps I am. Mexico is currently at war with the drug gangs, the mafia, and other violent and vile outlaws—a war for the hearts, lives, and souls of men. This is a spiritual battle. Satan is not holding anything back in this battle. He is fighting to win. We must give it our all. We must fight the good fight. We must be found faithful in our service for the King of kings and the Lord of lords.

I have always said that I would be willing to give my life or anything else for the cause of Christ.

This past year God has called me, repeatedly, to lay down things that I never thought would be required of me. It has not been easy, but God has called me to stand for righteousness and justice—even when those closest to me do not understand. There are days when my heart screams, "Please understand! I am not crazy. Even when you do not understand my thoughts and actions, I am not crazy!" We are in a spiritual warfare for the souls of our Mexican brothers and I refuse to sit and do nothing.

Nearly two decades ago the Lord began a work in the hearts and lives of families in diverse locations throughout Mexico. In the ensuing years deep friendships were born, grew, and prospered.

After announcing in June that we were taking a year off the work with the conferences and publishing the magazine, some had come to an incorrect conclusion about our continued work in Mexico.

Pam and I are not leaving Mexico!

We continue to work fervently for the Lord in and through *La Iglesia de Baratillo* and *Vida Nueva Ministries*; we continue to evangelize the lost; we continue to love and to support the home education work in Mexico and beyond. We continue to pray for and to look for creative ways to help and encourage families. The Lord has simply redirected and refocused our efforts. He has called us to do hard things for him—to be different—to stand and fight for right and justice in a society where few really find it.

A profound desire to do the will of the One whom we serve must become the ultimate reason for doing the things that we do, for going the places that we go, for saying the things that we say. Please pray for us. Pray that, above all, we would be found faithful in our service for the King of kings.

I have a life that is worth living and I desire more than anything to live it in a way that leaves an eternal impact on those around me. I am tired. I am weary but I am not defeated. I fight on, attempting to be a light in the midst of the darkness.

One day, as I was driving out of the town and getting ready to pull back on the highway, a car pulled up beside me. Five armed men were in the vehicle. I knew that I would be stopped. I feel prepared for them most of the time. Yet they still seem to catch me by surprise. I looked at my passengers and said—well, before I tell you what I said, let me tell you that now I can think of hundreds of spiritual remarks that I could have made at that moment.

What I said was … "Oh, no!" That is it—just "Oh, no!"

I knew I had to think quickly. I grabbed a handful of the booklets that I published especially for the people in that area and hopped out of the car to confront them eye to eye. I quickly began talking with them about the Lord and started handing them the booklets. After I gave two of them booklets the driver said, "We have got to go." I was barely able to get the booklets for the other three out before they drove off and left me standing on the side of the road. Seeds were planted that day that could not have been planted in any other way. The Gospel went forth and I praise God that He allowed me to be a little part of that process in that area that was filled with members of the drug cartel.

Satan and his evil forces have brought this fight to the Believers in Mexico. In Philippians 1:12-14, Paul told us that his chains caused his fellow Believers to become bolder in their testimony for the Lord. His captivity inspired them to preach the Word without fear.

There are literally thousands upon thousands of people near us who are struggling with the traumatic events that surround us. They are looking for answers. We, the Believers, have the answers that they need.

One day I had just finished working on a message for the church—a call to missions—a call to reach the lost no matter what the cost. Here is an excerpt from that message, "We must go to places of danger, places where there are many people open to the Gospel. We must fulfill our task of bringing the message of the cross to the people who are suffering here in this country. There are no exceptions for us as Believers. We must work faithfully to reach the world by reaching individuals for Christ."

Later that evening there was a major cartel battle in Miguel Aleman. The local townspeople told me that close to seventy people were killed in the battle. Miguel Aleman is right on the border of the USA and is eight miles north of Ciudad Mier.

In the last year, we have personally placed nearly 10,000 booklets and 900 Good and Evil books into the hands of soldiers and civilians. Because of the books and booklets being high quality, they are read! This fact has been confirmed repeatedly by comments, as well as requests for copies to share with friends and family. Sharing printed material that is of superior quality, not only in content but also in appearance, demonstrates to the people the value of the message that is printed on its pages and also shows them the value that we as Believers place on getting that message to them.

I stopped at the same gas station where I had given out some books the week before. Two workers came over to the truck. One man, whom I recognized, said that the other man had seen him reading the Good and Evil book that I had given him. He asked if I had another copy that I could give to his friend. Although I did not have any with me at the time, I told him that I would bring him one next week. Then I gave both of them a copy of a different booklet.

As I was getting ready to leave, the first man came back. He pointed to a third worker who was reading the booklet intently. Then he told me that his coworker was very interested in the booklet, so he gave him his copy. He asked me if he could get one more copy for himself. Just then, the second man came back to the truck and began talking with me about spiritual issues. Later, when I arrived home, Abigail, our youngest, came running up to me, arms outstretched, squealing, "Daddy's home—Daddy's home." Everything within me cried out, I have a life worth living!

Following months of intense, debilitating pain, I went to Monterrey looking for answers. I thought I was prepared for anything. I must admit, I was not.

My friend César helped me find the best doctors. He also attended all the appointments with me. On my way to pick up the MRI results, I was telling him that I thought the results would be better than the previous MRI that had been done years ago. When I read the results, I wept. I was ready for anything but a worsening of the Multiple Sclerosis!

Several days later, another MRI was ordered to see if I had lesions in the spinal area. By this time, I had accepted the advancement of the MS and decided after many years of not taking the normal medications for MS that it would be appropriate to try to take them. However, after the neurologist saw the abnormalities in the MRI, he sent me that day to the surgeon and told me not to worry about treating the MS until this issue was taken care of.

The Ankylosing Spondylitis took me by surprise. Once again, I wept. The Spondylitis has caused bone growth which caused a curving of the spine and swelling of the spinal column. The only way to solve it was surgery. While the doctor was looking at the MRI, he made a surprised sound. When I asked him why, he told me that four of my vertebra looked like what he would expect to see in a much older man. Due to the reduced size of the opening in the vertebra there was almost no spinal fluid flowing around four of my vertebra. Three doctors have said that this is an urgent situation. I had the operation three weeks later.

I have been told to wear a collar at all times, not to stand very long, to sit when I preach, not to climb stairs more than twice a day, not to drive, and — well, the lists for "nots" goes on and on, but you get the idea.

The health issues that I have been facing are multifaceted and complex. In addition to the MS and the need for spinal surgery, I was diagnosed with gout and psoriatic arthritis. Tests have also shown that there is little communication in the nerves between my knees and feet. For many months, I was able to walk with a walker.

There have been what appeared to be some bad days. There have been days that I cried. Nevertheless, there is a way to turn a bad day around! There is a way to find victory and be a conqueror — to be more than a conqueror. We must be willing to go up the mountains to be able to experience what God wants for our lives. Crossing the valley and climbing the mountain may be difficult but those are places and precious moments in our lives of intimacy with God. That is where you see God's power, and that will produce changes and will bring blessings.

On the mountain, or better said, on the way up the mountain, you will be able to see God's power, and this will produce changes in you. It will bring blessings, and you will see the glory of God. On the way up the mountain God will restore, comfort, exhort, and edify. God's invitation to His people has always been, "Come up and know Me." Go up the mountain and your life will never be the same. There is only one difference between our spiritual mountains and our valleys: that is our attitude!

Let us believe, let us truly believe, in the deepest place in our hearts that God is using the difficult situations for our good. If we believe so, then our valleys will become our mountains in an instant.

Before going into the hospital for surgery, I had one thousand booklets printed about overcoming bitterness, which I took with me to the hospital. I also took some boxes of Good and Evil. My plan was to talk to anyone who would listen, as I had the strength.

After the surgery, I could not get out of bed, but I also thought that there were more hurting people at the hospital than anywhere I know. Therefore, I came up with a plan—to encourage other Believers to get involved. Many Believers came to visit me. So I asked every one of them to take a few booklets and Good and Evil books and to talk with a few patients and their families before they left the building. I had been trying to reach hurting and dying people in many parts of this country but God used this situation to bring them to me!

My son Michael, my mom, and my stepfather all made tremendous sacrifices to come and spend time with me during the surgery and my recuperation. It was nice to spend the time with them.

I am grateful that I am now walking again and nearly pain free. Fatigue is still an issue as well as a few other MS-related symptoms.

Over the last year, Satan has attacked our family time and again, but the last five months have been different. He has pulled out all stops and brought in his legions of demons. He has surrounded my home and attacked with everything he had in his power. It is only by the grace of God that I am standing in the gap. My family and I have taken many hits and, yes, we are hurting. Satan overlooked two points when he decided to attack the Richardsons. First and foremost, he overlooked the fact that greater is He who is in us than he who is in the world. However, he also forgot about his last attack—my legs, my neck, and the most intense pain that I have ever seen. Yes, Satan brought that into my life, but God used it for my good. With God's help, I withstood more physical pain than most; I came through that attack different. I was beaten but not broken—but it was only because I learned from where my strength came from—God and His Word.

Satan has attacked yet again and it hurts. It has become necessary to stand firm and to stand strong. It has been necessary to pick up the spiritually wounded and carry them through the heat of the battle. Yes, this is harder than anything I have ever experienced before. Nevertheless, I will not give up. I will not fail. The stakes are too high. Lives and souls literally hang in the balance. I, along with my family, must face this battle. I have spent months working directly with police and prosecutors trying to end some of the worst kinds of evil here in Mexico. It has been hard, but God is good.

People are repenting and church services have been sweet. God is working in my life, my family, and the church here in Mexico. Revival is happening and even greater revival is on its way. I feel it everywhere I go. This country is ripe and ready for the harvest. God is preparing the Believers here to get out and do the work. I believe that a major part of this preparation had to do with me. God has broken every aspect of my heart. For years, I have been a prideful man who was of little real use for the Kingdom. God has brought me low so that I could see the real inner man. Yes, He broke me, but then He used the pieces to form a different man—one who understood that he could do nothing good within himself. I am now a man who has been sifted and purified—not perfect but truly seeking God's best in every aspect of my life. I am trying to sift every thought, every action, every attitude, and every decision through the words of 1 Corinthians 13.

I must admit, the process has been hard. Nevertheless, I can say that it has been worth it—I am changed, I am free. I am free within myself and I am free to serve God with a whole heart—with every ounce of my being—not just with the leftovers. I do not know what tomorrow or next week or next month will bring but I look forward to them with great anticipation. God has been good to me.

2 Chronicles 16:9 says, "For the eyes of Jehovah run to and fro in all the whole earth to show Himself strong on behalf of those whose heart is perfect toward Him." Everything within me is crying out, I want to be that man! God, help me be that man!

A man's joy and peace are not determined by his outward condition but by what is in his heart.

One morning, sitting in the silence of a bedroom, I began to pray. Is it not amazing how hurt and pain forces us to our knees? The Lord gently reminded me about a sermon that I preached: "The Joy of the Lord." I stood in pain before the congregation and said, "Rejoice in the Lord always. Again I say, Rejoice!" (Philippians 4:4).

Now God is whispering in my heart, in the stillness and quietness of the night, "Can you have joy? Can you demonstrate joy to all of those around you—even during painful and trying circumstances?"

Do I have what it takes to be joyful—really joyful? Or will I do like many people—snap and gripe at those closest to me, then put on a "happy face" when others are around?

The joy of the Believer should not depend only on the present circumstances but also on the things to come. We have a living hope set before us and we rejoice in that hope. To achieve true joy, we have to have a single mind—a mind that is not divided—a mind set on things above.

When I prayed, I asked the Lord to give me His joy and His peace. I wanted to ask Him to make things better—for Him to make this pain go away—but I did not, I could not. I desire more than anything to have the real joy of the Lord. Joy that busts forth, like a flower on a spring morning; a joy that nothing can hold back! That is the joy that I want—a joy that depends only on my relationship with God.

Have You Ever Had a Bad Day?

Your family will have trials and struggles just like my family. While the problems and difficulties in your life will be different from those that my family experiences, they do have one thing in common. You must learn to lean upon the Lord. He is able to carry the weight when you cannot. He will see you through every one of the challenges that you face. You can depend upon that.

For sinners, the bad days only get worse, but what about us—the Believer? Have you ever had a bad day? I have had many days that seemed like bad ones. I have had months when things seemed to go from bad to worse.

The sinner cannot expect that things will get significantly better. The prophet Amos describes the wicked as a man who flees from the lion and is met by a bear, who finally gets home, worn out, leans his hand on the wall, and is bitten by a snake.

For a child of God, a bad day is only the preparation for better days to come. God is the One who has the last word.

> For His anger is but for a moment, His favor is for life; weeping may endure for a night, but joy comes in the morning.
>
> —Psalm 30:5

For the Believer, God can make all things work together for good. A promise of God for His children is written in John 16:33: "These things I have spoken to you, that in Me you may have peace. In the world you will have tribulation; but be of good cheer, I have overcome the world."

Victory over the bad days can be reduced to this simple equation: Prayer plus praise equals deliverance. For this reason, the psalmist says. "From the rising of the sun to its going down the LORD's name is to be praised" (Psalm 113:3).

God was making all things, even the bad ones, work together for good.

Have you been going through bad days this week? Maybe you feel you had a bad year. It is possible that there are people who think they have had a bad life. It is time to change that. It is time to come out of the darkness and walk into the marvelous light of the Lord. Do not live a defeated life. Do not be depressed or discouraged. There is a way to turn a bad day around. There is a way to find victory and be more than a conqueror. Why do you not let go of that attitude of defeat? Let go of it today!

I think it would be good to meditate on the words of the first chorus that I learned in Spanish: "I am Yours."

> I am nothing and from the dust I was born, but You love me and died for me.
> Before the cross I can only exclaim:
> I am Yours. I am Yours.
>
> Take my hands, I beg You; take my lips, I love You;
> Take my life, O Father, I am Yours.

> Take my hands, I beg You, take my lips, I love
> You;
> Take my life, O Father, I am Yours, I am Yours.
>
> When on my knees I look at You, Lord, I see Your
> greatness and my littleness.
> What can I give You?
> Only my being. I am Yours, I am Yours.
>
> Take my hands, I beg You; take my lips, I love
> You;
> Take my life, O Father, I am Yours.
> Take my hands, I beg You; take my lips, I love
> You;
> Take my life, O Father, I am Yours. I am Yours. I
> am Yours.

Let us rid ourselves of our pride and of our selfish desires. Let us lay aside sin and focus on the cross. That is the road to becoming men and women useful to God. That is the road to becoming men and women used by God.

In the Bible we find that in the mountains, God manifests Himself to His servants. We must be willing to strive for that mountaintop experience with God. Crossing the valley and climbing the mountain may be difficult. Nevertheless, those are places and precious moments in our lives of intimacy with God. There you will be exposed to God's power, and this will produce changes in you that will bring blessings.

> Oh, send out Your light and Your truth! Let them
> lead me; let them bring me to Your holy hill and
> to Your tabernacle.

> —Psalm 43:3

On the mountain, or better said, on the way up the mountain, you will be able to see God's power which will produce changes in you. It will bring blessings and you will see the glory of God. On the way up the mountain God will restore, comfort, exhort, and edify. God's invitation to His people has always been, "Come up and know Me."

The mountain is a place for new beginnings. The mountain is a place where your calling begins. The mountain is a place for commitment and provision. The mountain is a place for revelation, meeting and fulfillment of promises.

Just as Moses did, go up the mountain and receive His commands, promises, correction, inheritance, so you may be the spiritual man or woman that God desires to make you. Go up the mountain and your life will never be the same.

One day, when my friend César and I were coming out of a doctor's office, we could hear music playing in the background. The receptionist told us that it was controlled by the hospital's main office. Nevertheless, in that precise moment God had worked things out so that the song that was playing was, "You Raise Me Up."

> When I am down and, oh my soul, so weary;
> when troubles come and my heart burdened be;
> then, I am still and wait here in the silence, until
> You come and sit awhile with me.
>
> You raise me up so I can stand on mountains; You
> raise me up to walk on stormy seas; I am strong
> when I am on Your shoulders; You raise me up to
> more than I can be.
>
> You raise me up so I can stand on mountains; You
> raise me up to walk on stormy seas; I am strong
> when I am on Your shoulders; You raise me up to
> more than I can be.
>
> There is no life—no life without its hunger; each
> restless heart beats so imperfectly; But when You
> come and I am filled with wonder, sometimes, I
> think I glimpse eternity.
>
> You raise me up so I can stand on mountains; You
> raise me up to walk on stormy seas; I am strong
> when I am on Your shoulders; You raise me up to
> more than I can be.
>
> You raise me up so I can stand on mountains; You
> raise me up to walk on stormy seas; I am strong

when I am on Your shoulders; You raise me up to
more than I can be.
You raise me up to more than I can be.

At that moment, I began to cry because God was telling me that
He would raise me up on my feet over the mountains of Arteaga.
He will raise me up when everything seems to be going from bad
to worse. I am strong if I am on His shoulders. He will raise me up.

Yes, I was struggling. Yes, I had physical difficulties. Nevertheless, when I am weak, God is strong in me.

When you feel like you cannot go on, then you are approaching
the point of being able to be useful for God. When you feel the
burden is too hard to carry, at that moment you have to turn and
look at God and when you remain with your eyes set on Him, you
will be able to be used by Him.

Our valleys can become mountains. God is good—all the time.
When everything goes well, God is good. When everything goes
wrong, God is good, because God is good.

May I suggest that there is only one difference between our
mountains and our valleys? That is our attitude. Let us believe, in
the deepest place in our heart, that God is using the difficult
situations for our good. If we believe so, then our valleys will
become our mountains in an instant.

Yes, I had strong pain in my body. Nevertheless, day by day I
have seen God working in my life and in the lives of those around
me. I had the opportunity to embrace my children, Anna and
Joshua, and to say to them, "God is good." I had the opportunity to
see Samuel seeking a solution like a man would. Pam had the
opportunity to see Isaac crying out to God. However, the blessings
are not limited to my family.

The Lord gave me the opportunity to speak to three doctors
about God and His greatness. He also gave me the opportunity to
pray with two of them. Without the pain, these things would never
have been possible. I am convinced that I am not the only person
who has suffered pain. Maybe your pain is also physical. Perhaps
you have a spiritual or an emotional pain—a pain no one can see. It
is possible that you hurt deeply inside and are storing resentment
in your heart.

God can and wants to take all those "valleys" in your life and turn
them into "mountains"—into victories—into victory upon victory.
You do not have to live sad and in low spirits. God is the answer.

Yes, it is true that sometime God's way can lead us to a place of pain. When Christ was in the world, His path took Him to the cross but He never lost His peace, His joy, or His relationship with God the Father.

He, and only He, can give you His peace and joy while you walk through dark valleys. When you really understand this from the bottom of your heart, you will no longer walk in the valley because God will have changed your valley into a mountain.

If you find yourself in despair today, financial or otherwise, turn to God. He will raise you up. Let Him show you the path that you need to take. Trust Him and He will give you peace no matter what your circumstances.

There is freedom from financial bondage, but more importantly, there is freedom in a relationship with Christ.

Chapter 18

Final Thoughts

George Müller has been an example to many in the handling of finances and in placing one's faith completely in God. But there is another way that that his life was a shining example. Sadly, few ever speak about it or even know about it. This was his balanced family life.

Yes, that is right! Müller was a man of God. He was a man of faith, and he maintained a balanced family life! Take a moment to meditate on this quote from The Mission-Minded Family by Ann Dunagan:

> "At his wife Mary's funeral, Müller's loving words also represent a good example of the joy God gives when ministry and family priorities are balanced:
> 'Were we happy? Verily we were.
> With every year, our happiness increased more and more. I never saw my beloved wife at any time, when I met her unexpectedly anywhere in Bristol, England, without being delighted so to do. Day by day, as we met in our dressing room, at the

Orphan Houses, to wash our hands before dinner
and tea, I was delighted to meet her, and she was
equally pleased to see me. Thousands of times I
told her, "My darling, I never saw you at any time,
since you became my wife, without my being delighted to see you.'"

It is not only my prayer that God will bless your finances as you
commit the handling of them to Him, but that God will bless you
and your family as you seek a deep, intimate relationship with Him
and each other.

In the days, weeks, and months to come, you will be making
decisions that will dramatically affect your life as well as the lives
of those around you. If you want to increase your usefulness in the
Kingdom of God, then you will learn to filter every decision
through His Word as well as mold your heart and your life to His
character. Use your life to serve the Lord with everything within
you. Give Him your all. Do not hold anything back.

Vida Nueva Ministries

1001 S 10th ST, Suite G529
McAllen Texas 78501
770-713-9053
Website: www.VNMinistries.org
General Information: Support@vnministries.org.
Mike Richardson: Mike@vnministries.org.

If you are interested in learning more about the Richardson family, *Vida Nueva Ministries*, *El Hogar Educador*, the Family Camp, or *La Iglesia de Baratillo*, visit our website at www.VNMinistries.org or write 1001 S. 10th St., Suite G529, McAllen, Texas 78501.